PRAISE FOR 7 STEPS TO COURAGE

Honest. Transparent. Vulnerable. Courageous. Encouraging. Insightful. These are some of the words that came to my mind as I read my friend Ann White's book. This book is going to bless and help a lot of people.

Daniel L. Akin, President
Southeastern Baptist Theological Seminary
Wake Forest, NC

Ann White's story is an inspiration to those who choose to do the hard things in marriage, rather than take the easy way out. This demonstration of one wife's courageous determination to trust God's truth, bathed in His grace, prove trust and obedience can overcome the deceiver who delights in crushing Christian marriages..

Governor Sonny and Mary Perdue
The State of Georgia

Sometimes all it takes is one small step to change your life forever. Ann White's small step will encourage countless readers to step out in faith and be courageous! If you are in need of courage today, Ann's practical, Word-inspired *7 Steps to Courage* can help you discover, as she did, a life you never dreamed possible! Get out your highlighter—this is one of those books you'll refer to again and again. I know I will.

Kimberley Kennedy
TV Journalist
Author of *Left at the Altar*

Men and women in marriages worldwide suffer in silence. They wear a mask in public and in front of family and friends. Issues may be what some would call minor, yet the man and woman in that marriage are suffering. Issues may be physically and emotionally damaging, yet the injured parties suffer in silence. Everyone is not called to share their 'dirty laundry' publicly, but some are called to share their story as a testimony to others that they are not alone and that there is hope for change and healing. I applaud Ann White and her family for courageously sharing what could have remained a quiet suffering followed by the hard work of change and the joy of healing. Ann's story is personal, painful, healing, and full of hope for anyone who suffers in silence. *7 Steps to Courage* is a powerful resource for pastors and counselors who are in the trenches with individuals and couples who are fighting for their marriage, and it is a personal lifeline to individual readers suffering in silence.

Stacy Robinson
TheRobinsonAgency.com
StandYourGroundMovie.com
TheChristianView.tv

Few are as qualified to write on the subject of courage as Ann White due to the fact that she has personally lived the principles she teaches. Allow Ann to help you be courageous rather than dismayed. On a personal note, I watched these truths lived out in her marriage.

Dr. Johnny Hunt
First Baptist Church
Woodstock, GA

I just finished *7 Steps to COURAGE*, and I have to tell you that God convicted and challenged me on several levels. Our family is going through a tough struggle right now (as all families do), and I intend to appropriate the truth into my life that jumped out at me from your book. Thank you for having the courage to open up and share your story in this way. I encourage and challenge everyone who is going through difficulties in their lives or relationships to read this book, and they will find truth straight from God's Word presented in a way that will inspire, convict, and move you from fear to courage, then to freedom and joy

Billy Goodwin

Newsong

In a world starving for authenticity, Ann White had the courage to be transparent with her story so that you too could walk in genuine courage. Her book, *7 Steps to Courage*, will guide you to live in truth with strength and dignity.

Kathrine Lee

Life & Business Strategist

Founder of Pure Hope Foundation

I have had the privilege of knowing Ann and her husband, Mike, who I consider very dear friends. I've had many conversations with them about our faith and struggles with turning our fears over to God. This book is a true testimony of overcoming the struggles that have been real in Ann's life. As I read it I was truly encouraged. I can honestly say this is a must-have book for your home or office library. And I can promise it is a must-read for everyone, whether or not you're struggling. God bless you, Ann, for sharing your struggles and your *7 Steps to Courage*.

Daryle Singletary

American Country Music Artist

7 STEPS TO
C♥URAGE

Ann White

with
Allison Bottke

CREATIVE ENTERPRISES STUDIO

BEDFORD, TEXAS

7 STEPS TO COURAGE

© 2016 Ann White

Published by Creative Enterprises Studio, 1507 Shirley Way, Suite A, Bedford, TX 76022. CreativeEnterprisesStudio.com.

Unless otherwise noted, Scripture quotations are taken from the NEW AMERICAN STAN-DARD BIBLE®, © The Lockman Foundation 1960, 1962, 1963, 1968, 1971, 1972, 1973, 1975, 1977, 1995. Used by permission.

Scripture quotations marked AMP are from the Amplified Bible. Copyright © 2015 by The Lockman Foundation, La Habra, CA 90631. All rights reserved.

Scripture quotations marked ESV are from the THE ENGLISH STANDARD VERSION. © 2001 by Crossway Bibles, a division of Good News Publishers.

Scripture quotations marked HCSB are from the Holman Christian Standard Bible. Copyright © 1999, 2000, 2002, 2003, 2009 by Holman Bible Publishers, Nashville Tennessee. All rights reserved.

Scripture quotations marked MSG are from the The Message by Eugene H. Peterson. © 1993, 1994, 1995, 1996, 2000. Used by permission of NavPress Publishing Group. All rights reserved.

Scripture quotations marked NIV 1984 are from the Holy Bible, New International Version®, NIV®. Copyright © 1973, 1978, 1984 by Biblica, Inc.™ Used by permission of Zondervan. All rights reserved worldwide. www.zondervan.com.

Scripture quotations marked NIV are from the Holy Bible, New International Version®, NIV® Copyright ©1973, 1978, 1984, 2011 by Biblica, Inc.® Used by permis¬sion. All rights reserved worldwide.

Scripture quotations marked NKJV are from THE NEW KING JAMES VERSION. © 1982 by Thomas Nelson, Inc. Used by permission. All rights reserved.

Scripture quotations marked NLT are taken from the Holy Bible, New Living Translation. © 1996. Used by permission of Tyndale House Publishers, Inc., Wheaton, Illinois 60189. All rights reserved.

Cover design and illustration by Carlos Magno Létes Rodrigues - http://CarlosMagno.me

Library of Congress Control Number: 2015958526

ISBN Softcover: 978-0989-0521-8-4

ISBN e-Book: 978-0989-0521-9-1

Printed in the United States of America

16 17 18 19 20 [MG] 6 5 4 3 2 1

To Mike

My soulmate and the love of my life

"With God All things are possible."

<small>MATTHEW 19:26</small>

Contents

Contents

Acknowledgments

*M*y sincere thanks to the many people who have helped make this book possible. First and foremost, I am eternally grateful to my Lord and Savior, Jesus Christ, for His gift of salvation and for the never-ending grace and love He gives me as I pray my way through life's many challenges and accomplishments.

I want to thank my sweet family for their love and support. For encouraging me to share with transparency my journey from fear to faith, from brokenness to courage. I am especially grateful to my husband, Mike, for fighting alongside me to save our twenty-nine-year marriage and to keep our family together. I am forever grateful for his love, forgiveness, mercy, and grace, and for encouraging and supporting me as I follow my God-given dreams.

Thank you to my wonderful sons for being the greatest sons a mom could ever want and for encouraging me to share my story with others. Thank you to my beautiful daughter-in-law, who is a special addition to our family. And to my adorable grandbabies, who brighten every day and constantly make me laugh.

To my brothers and sister, who love me and support my desire to help others by sharing with transparency my life journey. Thank you. And I want to thank my mom and dad, who currently reside in heaven, for loving me, providing for me, and for introducing me to the One who ultimately takes away

ACKNOWLEDGMENTS

our brokenness and makes us whole: Jesus. I look forward to our reunion in heaven that will be free from the struggles and the brokenness of this world.

A very special thank you to Allison Bottke, my writing coach and editor. Allison is not only a talented author but also a faithful woman of God who has the amazing ability to encourage people from all walks of life to turn away from destructive habits and pursue healthier, happier, faith-filled patterns in life. Thank you, Allison, for helping me polish every chapter of this book.

I am grateful for Robbie Goss, who counseled Mike and me through our crisis and who serves as our life coach and spiritual mentor to this day. I am thankful for his contribution to my life, my family, In Grace Ministries, and this book.

Thank you to Karen Kleinschmidt for being one of the first people to help me put my story into words. And to my amazing assistants, Kathy Sherwin and Melody Schmidt, thank you for putting up with my type-A personality and ADD. I couldn't get half as much done or do it nearly as well without your commitment to God and your dedication to me and In Grace Ministries.

A special thank you to all of my precious friends, too many to name, who not only held me up when I didn't have the strength to stand, but who stood firmly beside both Mike and me through the good, the bad, and the ugly. Who, to this very day, continue to offer unconditional love, encouragement, and a safe place where I can be transparent and vulnerable.

Finally, to you, the reader: thank you for taking time to read this book.

My prayer is that it encourages you and that the truth from this book gives you the courage to walk in newfound faith and freedom.

Introduction

The pressure of reality was closing in from all sides. It was as if the air was being sucked out of the room. As I tilted my head back in anguish, I felt like I was drowning in a sea of confusion and despair, and the only part of my body left above the surface was the tip of my nose. Without supernatural intervention, I was going under fast.

With shaking hands, I scribbled the current reality of my situation onto a sheet of hotel letterhead. It took me a few drafts before I got it right. When I finished, I called to confirm the intended recipients were in their room before I opened my door and headed out.

The hotel hallway felt like a dark tunnel closing in around me, and my footsteps whispered on the carpet as I walked in an almost trancelike state. Fear coursed through me. I had no idea what would happen next, only that I could no longer stay where I was.

How could this be happening to me? How would this truth be perceived?

Increasing doubts about lifting the veil of secrecy raced through my mind with each step.

For as long as I could remember, I had been afraid to let anyone see the real me. My secrets were like a dysfunctional security blanket I clung to for dear life. The night I mustered up the nerve to expose the truth, I finally said good-bye to that false sense of security—to the fearful isolation that had become my haven.

As strange as it seems, I didn't realize I lacked courage until I found it half-

INTRODUCTION

way around the world in a hotel room in Israel. On that night, I knew I had to take a major risk. Suddenly, I was like a hostage who had been held captive and finds herself with a window of opportunity to seek help—a sliver of time to reach out and let someone know she is in trouble.

As I walked and prayed, God gave me exactly what I needed in that moment: supernatural courage. Unbeknownst to me, I was taking the first step toward courage: Commit to Change. I was terrified, but I was resolute. It was now or never.

When my pastor's wife answered my knock, I all but shoved the note into her hands.

"I'm desperate and have to tell someone the truth. My marriage is on life support." The words quickly tumbled out as she stood there bewildered. Janet wasn't only my pastor's wife; she was a dear friend, the person who had planned a surprise birthday party for me just a few days before my adult son and I left for Israel. My husband and I had been friends with Johnny and Janet Hunt for over fifteen years, and they were about to learn that the marriage Mike and I portrayed was not what we lived.

"Come inside, Ann," she opened the door wider as I backed up.

"I can't . . . not now," I whispered, just as the elevator door opened a few feet from where we were standing and my pastor walked out. I wasn't ready to face him; I wasn't ready for a conversation with either of them. I was barely ready for what had just happened. But it had happened. And although I was shaking, I was still standing. I pushed through my fear long enough to invite someone else into my deepest struggle. I was no longer a hostage to the bitter truth. I awkwardly thanked Johnny and Janet, told them I had to go, and quickly rushed back down the hall to my room.

This was the moment I began my journey toward freedom. Not from any person, place, or thing, but from the bondage of my own fear-based choices.

Introduction

From the dark place of isolation where I felt so alone. This is where writing became the vehicle God used to give me courage and transport me to a place of amazing grace. And it all started on a sheet of hotel letterhead.

I didn't know what would happen once my husband (who had remained stateside) found out what I had done. But the truth that everything wasn't perfect in our life was at last coming out, and God was at work in miraculous ways. I took His Word to heart: "There is now no condemnation for those who are in Christ Jesus."[1]

Confessing the truth to Johnny and Janet started a chain reaction that led me toward honesty, openness, help, and healing. That night, I took the *C* and *O* steps in COURAGE as I committed to change and I overcame the obstacle of secrecy and isolation.

The Bible says, "Therefore, confess your sins to one another and pray for one another, that you may be healed. The prayer of a righteous person has great power as it is working."[2]

It was then I began to understand a powerful truth: when our actions and behaviors are based on unhealthy, fear-based choices, the relationships we have with others will never be healthy—whether it's with a spouse, family member, friend, employer, or even the person sitting next to us at church. I desperately wanted a healthy relationship with my husband, but that was never going to happen if the part I played wasn't truthful.

Exposed, Exhausted, and Exhilarated

For many of us, being in unhealthy relationships has become a way of life, whether it's in relationships with others or the one we have with ourselves. Many of us have resigned ourselves to the distorted belief that we are destined to exist in a kind of half-life, in a world where tension is normal and joy eludes us. We've come to believe that it is what it is.

INTRODUCTION

We've set the bar for happiness and joy extremely low.

Some of us, like me, have gone so far as to deny problems even exist, living in a fantasyland of dysfunction and isolation.

Some of us blame the people around us for making our lives miserable. But the truth is, it's not about the choices those around us make—although their choices can (and often do) affect us. When all is said and done, it's our own choices that really make all the difference, including how we choose to respond to the choices others are making.

What I'm saying isn't rocket science. It isn't advanced physics. But it is something that cripples countless men and women, no matter their level of intellect, success, or faith.

Finding the courage to foster healthy relationships is about the choices we make to change the story of our own lives. It's about praying for godly wisdom and discernment to accept responsibility for those choices, courage to face their consequences, and the strength to move on. And it's about the healthy boundaries we set—or don't set—for ourselves.

If you've spent any time pretending to be someone or something you aren't, you know how exhausting and isolating the dance can be. Contrary to what some may think, it takes a great deal of energy to hide behind a mask of fear and self-condemnation. Many of us have constructed the walls of our personal prisons so high and so strong, we've lost sight of who or what we are protecting ourselves from. All we know is that to expose who we really are is an unthinkable act with inconceivable consequences.

When I found myself in a hotel room in Israel contemplating divorce, I had no idea I was about to test-drive all seven of the courage steps. Steps I would begin to consistently follow, day after day, that would ultimately change my life. Steps that can also change yours, no matter what fearful situation you may be experiencing.

1

Finding Courage

Courage is taking a risk—not knowing the outcome.

"Be strong and courageous, do not be afraid or tremble at them, for the LORD your God is the one who goes with you. He will not fail you or forsake you."
—*Deuteronomy 31:6*

O ur young minds shape our belief systems about family, love, marriage, God, and life as we experience it. These beliefs, in turn, shape our choices and habits, both good and bad.

I learned as a child to blindly turn the other cheek and pretend everything in life was perfect, even when it was far from it. I grew up learning not to rock the boat, and I carried that dysfunctional coping mechanism into all of my relationships, particularly in my marriage.

Finding courage to change bad habits took me a long time.

Both of my parents were married to someone else when they met each other through work. My mother had two small boys and my father had a young son and daughter. They met, divorced their spouses, and married. Within two years, they had me. His, hers, and ours; we were the new modern family.

We were also monumentally dysfunctional, long before I knew what the word meant.

The father I knew was successful and a good provider, but he was also angry, self-absorbed, emotionally and verbally abusive, at times physically abusive, and consistently unfaithful. My mother worked hard to keep him calm and to accommodate his extreme behaviors. This shaped my distorted belief that a good wife accepts and accommodates the attitude, behavior, and choices of her husband—good, bad, or indifferent. I believed a good wife did not have her own identity.

But without a clearly defined sense of identity, we can allow ourselves to make poor choices and be overlooked and devalued.

God's desire is to enable us to make healthy choices that honor Him first and subsequently flow through us and into our relationships. He wants all of our relationships to be healthy, to come from places of truth. He wanted me to walk in power and purpose and wanted Mike and me to have a healthy, loving marriage.

However, none of those things would happen unless some major changes occurred. And when push came to shove, the only thing I could really change was me.

If you begin now to apply the 7 Steps to COURAGE, learning this natural progression of how to make healthy choices may not take you as long as it took me.

My prayer is that God will use the courage He gave me to help you find yours.

Finding Courage

CROSSROADS

I have never been compelled to write down my feelings. Not as a girl when I was given a little gold-clasped diary with a teeny-tiny key that never really worked, and certainly not as an adult when a Christian counselor advised me to journal as a way to sort through my mixed-up emotions. Writing has never been a place I aspired to go. Yet writing was a catalyst God used to help me take a stand and recover my lost identity, to force my hand toward honesty and, ultimately, toward healing.

And it was in God's Holy Land where He began to exert that pressure.

I was on a ten-day tour of Israel with my oldest son, Blake. It was a dream vacation where we would experience the Scriptures come to life with our pastor, his wife, and about forty other church members. We planned to visit some of the most breathtaking sites in the world. This should have been one of the happiest times of my life. But as day one came to an end, the only thing on my mind was that my twenty-six-year marriage was all but over.

It was a long day of touring an ancient seaport, a Roman theatre in Caesarea, and historic spots in Mount Carmel, Megiddo, and the Valley of Armageddon. I tried desperately throughout the day to keep my head up and hold on to my carefully crafted façade that everything was okay. No one questioned why my husband had remained in the States. Mike is a successful and well-respected businessman, and folks were accustomed to our unconventional life. In fact, several of my fellow travelers commented on how special it was that a mother and son could experience such a memorable vacation together. I agreed with them; it was special, and I so wanted to pretend the only thing that mattered was making lifetime memories with my twenty-four-year-old son. Yet truthfully, the waves of reality were crashing in all around me, and I was drowning.

3

I hoped this trip would be a nice reprieve from the escalating tension at home between my husband and me. We both hoped the time apart would be a good thing for our relationship, that it would allow us to cool off and take stock of the bigger picture. I even decided to leave my phone turned off in order to limit our communication.

When Blake's phone rang just as we returned to the hotel that first evening, I sat on the edge of the bed to untie my walking shoes and pretended not to listen as my son exchanged pleasantries with his dad and gave him highlights about our day.

"I'm going to my room to take a shower," I heard Blake say. "Do you want to talk to Mom? She's right here."

So much for leaving my phone turned off to avoid another confrontation.

I wasn't ready to talk to Mike, but I didn't want to put Blake in an awkward position either. We never wanted our boys to be aware of any problems between us, and we always did our best to shelter them from any challenges we were having.

After Blake disappeared through the door that connected our rooms, it didn't take Mike and me long to pick up where our last argument had ended, and even more hurtful words were spoken. For the next hour we rehashed everything broken in our relationship and how far we had grown apart. After almost three decades of marriage, we just couldn't seem to let go of our festering bitterness, mistrust, unforgiveness, and anger.

We were literally and figuratively thousands of miles apart that night as we tried to talk civilly about how we were going to end our marriage. But by the end of our conversation, we were simply in another fight—and hung up. Both of us were feeling completely defeated and hopeless.

Perhaps you know what hopelessness feels like. Maybe you are in the midst of a desperate battle to save a relationship or mourning over the loss of one.

Finding Courage

Maybe you are single and your need to find courage has nothing whatsoever to do with a significant other. Maybe you are at a crossroads in life, facing overwhelming odds, choices, or changes, and you find yourself drowning in fear.

No matter what you're going through, fear not. Courage is possible!

And with God's help, I'm going to help you find it.

The 7 Steps to COURAGE will bring you closer to the power of God, a supernatural power promised in His Word. "Now all glory to God, who is able, through his mighty power at work within us, to accomplish infinitely more than we might ask or think."[1]

WHAT IS COURAGE?

Courage is something most of us want. It's an attribute of integrity and good character that makes us worthy of respect. It gives us the ability to be brave, to conquer fear and despair.

When I was growing up, it was the boys who were taught to be strong, fearless, and courageous, not the girls. Especially not in my house, where I learned destructive patterns of codependency, denial, and isolation from my mother.

I recently saw this message on a church marquee: "What you tolerate, children emulate."

My mom tolerated a great deal, and as far back as I can remember, I viewed her way of coping as a valuable attribute, and I wanted to be just like her. I didn't understand how broken she was.

We bring so much past history into our present relationships, and not all of it is good.

There are different types of courage, ranging from physical strength and endurance to mental stamina and innovation. Courage can be defined in many ways, but I like this following list of definitions.

7 STEPS TO COURAGE

Courage means:

1. Taking a risk, not knowing the outcome

2. Trying something new

3. Saying yes to positive challenges

4. Making wise choices in the face of fear

5. Being honest with others and ourselves

6. Being able to admit we've been wrong

7. Accepting what we cannot change and changing what we can

8. Accepting God's view over all others

9. Giving grace to those who have hurt us

10. Choosing to persevere even when we're afraid

11. Choosing joy in the midst of all circumstances

Oliver Wendell Holmes said, "Courage is about doing what you're afraid to do. There can be no courage unless you're scared. Have the courage to act instead of react."

When we act, we are making a rational choice. Conversely, when we react, we are making an emotional choice. There's something to be said for maintaining a healthy balance between these two actions.

The 7 Steps to COURAGE I present in this book will provide the tools you need to learn how to act more than react, make intentional choices, experience the power of fearless choices, and find joy in the journey of healthy choices.

Finding Courage

Intentionally looking for courage and utilizing tools to make better choices is, in itself, a courageous act. It's an act I wish I had taken long before I reached the place where my lack of courage threatened virtually everything I held dear to my heart.

Kudos to you for reaching this place in your life now.

A 7-Step Journey

When we faithfully (and intentionally) implement the 7 Steps to COURAGE, the exercise will produce amazing results. It will strengthen our courage muscles and, ultimately, bring us into a closer relationship with our heavenly Father. And it's this relationship, above all others, that enables us to walk with courage, live in grace, and find true joy on the miraculous journey of life.

Get ready to unpack the steps I took to find the strength to make fearless choices. My prayer is that you, too, will feel convicted to follow these life-changing steps and find similar strength and freedom.

The 7-Steps to COURAGE:

C = **Commit** to Change

O = **Overcome** Obstacles

U = **Uncover** Our True Self

R = **Replace** Worldly Lies with Scriptural Truth

A = **Accept** the Things We Cannot Change

G = **Grasp** God's Love for Us

E = **Embrace** a Life of Grace

THE 7 STEPS TO COURAGE

Commit to Change

Overcome Obstacles

Uncover Your True Self

Replace Worldly Lies with Spiritual Truth

Accept the Things You Cannot Change

Grasp God's Love for You

Embrace a Life of Grace

© InGraceMinistries.org

A FAITHFUL FOCUS

There isn't a magical yellow-brick road that will lead us to a fearless place where we can instantly find courage. But God has provided us a way to hope and healing, a way to find saving grace and experience true joy.

My prayer is that you will find God's hope, healing, and grace in these pages.

As we move forward, I feel it's important to make it clear that my perspective on this topic is that of a courageous Christian woman. Although I invite readers of all faiths to learn how to make courageous choices, I believe a critical part of any enduring solution will be found in a firm trust in God along the way.

Finding Courage

God knows when our hearts are breaking. He knows the fear-based choices we make create open wounds that never seem to heal. But when we seek to please the Lord in all areas of our life, His desires will become the desires of our own heart. The Bible says, "Delight yourself in the LORD, and He will give you the desires of your heart." [2]

As I've trekked through the mud and mire of poor choice consequences, I've found the most direct route to courage and grace is to pray for wisdom and discernment to make God-directed decisions. When we seek His kingdom above all else, and live righteously, He will give us everything we need. [3]

Having courage is, in essence, all about making good decisions—God decisions.

Now, just so we are on the same page, this isn't necessarily an easy thing to do on a consistent basis. Especially when we've developed dysfunctional habits and coping mechanisms that have enabled us to operate for any length of time in a kind of spiritual or emotional amnesia. Or when people around us are making their own self-destructive choices.

It's difficult to manage life when the worldly lies we have come to believe have trapped us in a ditch of desperation, when we're feeling insignificant, insecure, and afraid.

Difficult, yes, but far from impossible.

The 7 Steps to COURAGE can help if any of these describe you:

- Have trouble saying yes and/or no with firmness and love
- Feel like no one understands what you are going through
- Have things in your past you are afraid to tell anyone about
- Have been betrayed by a close friend or someone you loved

- Struggle with unforgiveness

- Have developed unhealthy coping mechanisms (bad habits)

- Have experienced verbal, emotional, sexual, or physical abuse

- Are unhappy with your body image

- Struggle to accept that you are forgiven

- Feel confused about your identity or purpose in life

- Look for love in all the wrong places

LOOKING FOR LOVE

By many standards, Mike and I had an enviable life: two great kids, a lovely home, successful business, and active involvement in our church and community. There was no denying Mike and I loved each other. We had just made so many poor choices along the way. The fabric of our relationship was torn and tattered, in desperate need of repair, but neither of us really knew where, or how, to begin.

We were a mess, and maybe the most tragic part was nobody knew. We were so good at hiding the deterioration of our marriage, nobody had a clue how dangerously close we were to ending it. In fact, many viewed us as the perfect storybook couple.

I met Mike White on the first day of school at Milton High, shortly after my family moved to Georgia. Not knowing the social rules of my new school, I dressed up for my first day wearing a skirt, blouse, and heels. In the land of blue jeans, I stood out. Mike smiled at me and offered to walk me to class. A few months later, we both participated in a Christmas play, and that was it.

I was fourteen years old and on my way to being hopelessly in love.

Finding Courage

Mike was charismatic, warm, cute, upbeat, fun, and he was a senior. My lowly freshman status didn't seem to matter to him, and I found myself comfortably lost in his aura of confidence. Mike genuinely cared for me, and he regularly found ways to demonstrate his growing affection. He quickly became my savior in nearly every sense of the word, a role no human being should possess.

He helped me escape my family's brokenness, and he protected me from a frequently volatile dad. He made me look good and feel accepted. Mike gave me an identity. Over the years, he gave me two beautiful children and provided for us in ways I never dreamed possible.

What he couldn't give me was courage to take the growing stack of unhealthy, worldly lies I was constructing around myself—particularly the lie that any human being could ever meet all of my needs—and replace them with healthy, scriptural truth.

Mike couldn't help me make fearless, courageous choices. But in his defense, that wasn't his job.

It's no one else's job to help us make good choices and set healthy boundaries; that responsibility falls on our own shoulders. My husband was making choices based on his own belief system—on what he felt was right—not considering the emotional stability (or occasional instability) of his wife. That isn't to say he intentionally ignored or purposefully disrespected my feelings; he just didn't grasp the weight of responsibility I placed in his lap. Mike is an amazing man, but it's not easy to live up to savior status.

The fact that I came into our marriage with a boatload of boundary issues wasn't something either of us understood. I didn't comprehend (and certainly couldn't articulate) how I had developed a fear-based mentality as a child, why I had now grown into an adult controlled by fear and a detrimental need for acceptance, or how I could stop.

7 STEPS TO COURAGE

STOP THE INSANITY

It's time to learn how to stop. If we truly wish to find courage, we must intentionally get off the roller coaster and stop the endless cycle of ups and downs that occur when we make fear-based choices.

Fear is a natural emotion designed by God. But living with a spirit of fear is not from God.

If you are struggling with a challenging relationship, a difficult situation, or even with memories from a painful past, it's important to know God wants to give you courage to overcome this and any obstacle in life.

God wants to help us stop making fearful choices.

Although Mike and I both made poor choices over the years, my ability to find courage and walk in grace wasn't dependent on him acknowledging or accepting any part he played in the scenario. My ultimate freedom depended first and foremost on how willing I was to stop my own negative behaviors.

Ouch.

Yes, Mike's ability and willingness to accept responsibility for his choices was vital in our healing as a couple, but it's an important distinction to make that our ability to be hopeful and courageous is not dependent on the choices others may or may not make.

I was sitting in a hotel room in Israel when I took my first courage step, when I followed the Spirit-filled conviction to step out in faith and commit to change. I knew it was time for me to accept responsibility for my part in the dramatic dysfunction and own it. It was time for me to stop the insanity of repeating the same behavior and expecting different results. It was time for me to get off the gerbil wheel of insanity.

How about you? Is it your time to join me?

Finding Courage

A Phone Call Ends, a New Life Begins

The heated long-distance phone conversation I had with Mike that first night in Israel exhausted me. I sat on the hotel bed afterward and cried. In addition to feeling defeated and hopeless, I was distraught, depressed, and isolated.

It was in the midst of these overwhelming feelings when God, in His abundant mercy and grace, reached down to give me the supernatural courage I needed to follow a new path of change. This is when He convicted me to write the note that changed everything.

**Listen to the Holy Spirit. Is He convicting you now that something needs to change?

After I divulged our troubled marriage to our pastor and his wife, I didn't know how I was going to tell Mike. But I soon learned I didn't need to know, because God did, and He began to work almost immediately. After I delivered the note to Janet and got back to my room, Mike and I got back on the phone and I mustered the courage to tell him what I did. I felt unusually calm afterward, like a tremendous weight had been lifted. He wasn't happy, not by a long shot, but I think he sensed something had changed in my resolve. To his credit, Mike didn't retreat in anger, and by the end of our conversation, we actually began to proactively plan what was going to happen next. We agreed to see a counselor when I returned.

Our marriage wasn't miraculously healed overnight, but at least we were beginning to move in a healthier direction.

However, the feelings of exhilaration disappeared by the next morning. I tried really hard to act normal and happy, but in reality I was a nervous wreck and did my best to avoid Johnny and Janet. Even though my note prompted Mike and me to finally discuss seeking professional help as a couple, the fleeting courage I had the previous night was gone. Frankly, I felt terribly exposed and embarrassed. After finally coming clean, I wanted to hide, to disappear. I had no idea what to do or say. Do I act normal now? What does normal even look like? I didn't know how to act, and I felt guilty for dumping this issue on our friends.

What I really longed to do was go back into hiding and pretend everything was okay again.

But I couldn't; the truth was out and there was no taking it back.

Thank God.

During our first excursion of the day, I tried to remain as inconspicuous as possible, but my raw emotional state eventually bubbled to the surface. The experience of being in God's Holy Land was profound for many of us on the trip, so being overwhelmed with emotion didn't seem out of place as I walked away from the group at one point to try and compose myself. I think people likely assumed I was simply caught up in the moment.

It was then that my pastor and his wife found their own window of opportunity and reached out to privately offer words of wisdom and support.

"Ann, we love you and Mike. We will do whatever we can to help you both get the help you need. You're not alone."

We talked briefly before they returned to the group, and I began to comprehend that things would never again be the same.

After taking a few more minutes to compose myself, I rejoined our group with a fresh resolution to enjoy the time I had in Israel with my son and to absorb as much of God's truth as my heart and soul would allow.

A few days later, I was baptized in the Jordan River. As I stood in the same body of water that once covered my Savior, I knew the Spirit of God was washing me clean, reminding me I am not defined by my choices: "Therefore if anyone is in Christ, he is a new creature; the old things passed away; behold, new things have come."[4]

Finding Courage

While I knew I had a long way to go to heal from damaged emotions, I also realized God calls me His beloved, and to Him I am pleasing, no matter what mistakes I have made or how painful the memories are that threaten to destroy my peace and strangle my joy.

The Breakthrough

We live in an era where disposable relationships are acceptable—where going the distance is often viewed as a race far too difficult to run—particularly when the distance is fraught with gale-force winds. While this is true in all close relationships, it's especially true in marriage. Staying married these days, even in the best of times, isn't easy. Staying married when storms threaten is even harder.

Retreating from the torrential downpour of poor choices and painful consequences is often the easiest choice. Yet taking the easy way out isn't necessarily the wisest, or the healthiest, way out. Sometimes we have to jump boldly into the deep end of the pool to rescue what is important to us.

I thank God my husband is a bold man who was willing to jump.

That isn't to say he is a perfect man, any more than I am a perfect woman. We are both just children of a mighty God who know what it's like to struggle to keep our heads above water in order to survive. Just as we know what it feels like to see the shore of salvation in the distance.

It is through God's grace and mercy I have become a courageous woman. And I'm deeply blessed to be married to an equally courageous man who is also walking his own journey of faith, forgiveness, and grace.

It's impossible to describe the love and respect I feel for my husband as he has fought valiantly alongside me to restore "what the locust has eaten."[5] Although his personal journey is not mine to tell, I can tell you that on June 17, 2012, my husband rededicated his life to the Lord. I can tell you we are communicating in a way I never dreamed possible. And I can tell you we have both found the courage to change, through God's miraculous love, forgiveness, and grace.

One of the biggest challenges many of us who seek courage must overcome is our fearful need to hide and pretend. However, being courageous does not mean it's necessary to disclose our life history to everyone we meet.

While it's good to be transparent and vulnerable, there is a time and place for it.

As Mike and I continue to navigate new paths of honesty and trust on our journey as husband and wife, I respect Mike's request that we not divulge all of the particulars about our personal life in this book, just as he respects my choice to be as transparent and vulnerable as possible. Together, we are learning the value of balance in healthy disclosure.

My amazing husband and I are a walking testimony to God's saving grace. As we continue to heal, God is shaping and molding us into the individuals He wants us to be. He is teaching us what emotional triggers look like, how we can approach them in a healthy way, and how He wants us to use our experience to touch the lives of other broken couples and individuals.

Mostly, He is teaching us what forgiveness really looks like.

In her *Counseling Through Your Bible Handbook*, author June Hunt has this to say about one of the key areas in finding courage in all of our relationships in life:

Do choose as an act of will to forgive. Forgiving someone does not necessarily mean you must forget. The key is how the offense will be remembered. Forgiving is remembering without bitterness, hatred, or resentment. "Bear with each other and forgive whatever grievances you may have against one another. Forgive as the Lord forgave you" (Colossians 3:13 NIV 1984).[6]

Without a doubt, God's grace has enfolded me in a protective shield of love and forgiveness that has allowed me to walk in true purpose and experience a miraculous healing in my marriage.

God started me on the journey to find courage when my life and marriage was at their lowest point. Today, I continue to apply and demonstrate the 7 Steps to COURAGE, and my marriage is the strongest it has ever been. Is it perfect? No. There is no such thing as a perfect relationship, whether it's with a spouse, family member, or friend. The only perfect relationship we will ever have is with the Almighty, and because one-half of that couple will always struggle with worldly imperfections, even that relationship will forever be in stages of development. And that's how it should be. A personal relationship with our Creator is an organic entity that grows as we do, and the more we choose intimacy with God, the closer we will grow in understanding the kind of healthy intimacy He wants us to experience with Him, with ourselves, and with others.

Since I began to apply the 7 Steps to COURAGE, Mike and I have both grown closer to God and to each other. We are a miraculous work in progress; we are committed and we remain deeply in love. God continues to work in and on us.

UNITED IN COURAGE

The Hebrew word for courage is *hāzaq*, which literally means "to show oneself strong" and appears numerous times in Scripture. The Bible provides many rich examples of courage. Throughout God's Word, we see miraculous accounts of God accomplishing great deeds through ordinary people.[7]

7 STEPS TO COURAGE

As Mike and I continue our individual journeys walking with courage and living in grace, we have witnessed a miraculous change not only in our marriage but in all of our relationships. We've been able to move forward in restorative freedom, freedom that enables us to experience closeness and connection on a new level. We've grown stronger.

At the end of every chapter here you'll find several powerful exercises you can use to grow stronger courage muscles. The Courage Call-to-Action Steps will help you apply what you're learning in an intentional way. Never underestimate the long-term effects these short-term exercises can bring.

In the closing chapters, "Move Forward in Freedom" and "Find Joy in the Journey," we will transition from fearful brokenness to courageous wholeness.

Join me in discovering a world of strong faith and amazing freedom, a place where you can be fully known, fully understood, and fully loved, right where you are. A place where you can uncover hurt, tackle healing, and embrace victory.

Together, we will find the courage our souls desperately long for. We will stand firm, not be hampered, and not be weighed down by the burdens the world seeks to place on us. As fellow warriors, we will learn how to lay aside our heavy loads in order to take up Christ's yoke that is far lighter. Together, we will learn how to make fearless choices and walk in grace.

Together, we will find the courage to change our lives.

COURAGE CALL-TO-ACTION STEPS

1. Purchase a spiral notebook or some type of blank journal. Put your name and the date on the first page. Keep this notebook nearby as you read to jot down thoughts, tips, and Scripture notes.

2. Take a few minutes to write down how you are feeling after reading this chapter. List the areas in your life where you might need to make more courageous choices.

3. Draw a vertical line down the center of one page in your notebook and use these column headers: Courage and Fear. Now, take a self-inventory and in the appropriate column, list the ways you exhibit courage and/or fear. There are no right or wrong answers. This is a stream-of-consciousness exercise designed to break down barriers and open the floodgates of forgiveness.

2

Navigating Toward Change

Courage is trying something new for the very first time.

*"Behold, I am doing a new thing; now it springs forth, do you not perceive it?
I will make a way in the wilderness and rivers in the desert."*
—*Isaiah 43:19,* ESV

A few days before my trip to Israel, I agreed to join Mike for dinner with a business client. We were barely talking, but I convinced myself we could at least get through dinner.

But when Mike opened the restaurant door, I walked into a surprise birthday party for me hosted by our dear friends Janet and Johnny. The entire restaurant was filled with friends and family.

I was completely humbled to be loved by so many people. Yet no one realized that night how broken I was, how much energy it took me to not turn and run.

But instead of running, I donned my party mask.

I mustered up all the pretend strength and fake courage I had and put on a happy face.

Once again, I was able to cover up what was truly going on in my life from everyone who knew and loved me, just like I had done since I was a little girl.

In retrospect, I can see how Mike also donned appropriate masks over the years. For example, although our communication had rapidly deteriorated in the weeks leading up to this party, Mike didn't want to tell our friends about our situation and spoil all the plans they made, so he, too, pretended everything was fine. We were the king and queen of deception and illusion.

The main problem was that in addition to deceiving others, we had lost ourselves in the process.

When we ignore our emotions and needs, or pretend our pain and problems don't exist, our feelings of fear, depression, or despair are likely to increase. Chances are, that may be what has driven you to seek a resource to help you find the courage to make positive changes in your life, changes that will not only impact your relationships but your entire future.

In that hotel room in Israel, when I made the commitment to change, I had no idea it would be the first step on my journey to find courage. I had no idea it would inevitably lead me to a place where I could learn how to make fearless choices. At the time, I desperately longed to find joy in my world, but I had never felt further from it.

I wasn't sure how to stop all of my negative habits, but hopefully someone else did. That's why I had to break the suffocating silence that kept me in isolation. I had to tell someone that my life and my marriage were falling apart. I had to let someone know I was barely treading water, and if help didn't arrive soon I would drown.

Navigating Toward Change

CHANGING COURSE

The Bible says, "Do not be conformed to this world, but be transformed by the renewing of your mind."[1] When we begin to navigate toward change, we are really taking the first step to renewing our mind.

It is possible to shift our thinking, learn new values, and change our thoughts, attitudes, and behavior. It is possible to change course, no matter our circumstances or age. And this can be as easy, or as difficult, as we choose to make it.

Once we come to the place where we are ready to commit to change, we need to ask ourselves, *How can I prepare myself to handle change?* and *What will I need to accomplish in order to maintain my commitment to change?*

For me, I had to learn how to change inappropriate attitudes, behaviors, beliefs, circumstances, coping skills, desires, and emotions. I had to learn how to intentionally act instead of emotionally react. I had to be prepared to accept the consequences of my new choices.

And I had to lean heavily on my relationship with God and trust His Word for wisdom and guidance.

When we decide to take the bold step of navigating toward change, it is comforting to know we don't have to take the journey alone. I remember feeling as though I was setting off into uncharted waters, not knowing if I was going to sink or sail. I felt like the biblical Peter: brave but afraid, trusting but questioning, walking on water one minute and sinking below the surface the next.

Jesus, walking on the sea in the midst of gale-force winds, came toward the disciples and asked them to take courage and not be afraid. Jesus then commanded Peter to step out of the boat and onto the raging sea, the same sea that was battering the boat he and his fellow disciples were holding on to for dear life. Peter, having faith he could do Christ's will with Christ's help, took a giant leap of faith. He placed one leg and then the other over the side of the plank-board boat, stepped out onto the water, and began making his way to Jesus. But, being human, Peter took a few steps in faith and then heard the voice of doubt in his mind, and in that split second, he chose to listen to that voice that began to recite a familiar tune: *Are you crazy? You can't do this! You're going to get hurt; you are much better off to stay right where you are!*[2]

Oh, how I can relate to Peter. How about you?

Whether our inner voices whisper, cajole, or scream, there's no doubt we listen to them.

As soon as Peter took his eyes off Christ and focused on the bad things that might happen, he began to sink.

Can we really choose to tune out these inner voices of doubt?

I believe we can.

With consistent and intentional training, we can take the inner voices that accuse, judge, and threaten and override them with voices that empower, encourage, and support.

In learning to make courageous choices, I've found it critical to keep my eyes on Christ, "the source and perfecter of our faith."[3] Unless I completely trust the loving arms of my Savior to hold me when the waters get rough, I will be forever susceptible to listening to my inner judge or accuser, who is constantly standing by just waiting to bury me in fear.

We live in a sinful world, and there will always be a destructive inner voice telling us we can't handle the process of changing critically unhealthy parts of our life. An inner voice that wants to stunt our growth in every way and keep us in bondage to fear.

It's not always easy, but we can choose not to listen to that voice.

Navigating Toward Change

Preparing for Change

Pain is often a common partner of change. As we begin our journey to find courage, it's helpful to do our best to understand this profound truth: sometimes God allows pain to motivate us toward change.

It's also helpful to set aside ample time for reflection and prayer. Ask God to give you wisdom and discernment to make healthy, courageous choices that honor Him.

It's been said that we resist change until the pain of staying the same becomes greater than the pain of change.

Many of us know we need to change, but we hesitate out of pain, fear, uncertainty, or simply being stuck in negative patterns of behavior. For me it was all of the above, and God had to bring me to the point of a complete crisis to motivate me to make necessary changes in my life, changes that included a lot of soul-searching, prayer, and intentional choices.

When we decide to commit to change, it's important to act intentionally/rationally, and not react impulsively/emotionally. This is a finite distinction we must learn: the critical difference between acting and reacting.

The readier, willing, and able we are to respond rationally when we experience the emotional pain that often accompanies change, the more successful we will be in staying on course when the course gets rough.

Setting Healthy Boundaries

To walk in true freedom, many of us need to identify why we have allowed things to reach the messed-up point they have, and stop focusing on the part someone else played in getting us here. For many of us, it's time to shine healing light on our own boundary-related identity issues.

7 STEPS TO COURAGE

The subject of boundaries will come up often in these pages, as will the issue of understanding our identity. There is a common denominator in these two areas centered on self-worth, self-respect, and self-esteem issues.

For the most part, we are in control of the choices we make. A significant aspect of finding courage is gaining a better understanding of why we make our choices. And one of the deciding factors in our ability to make good choices has a lot to do with what we know and believe about boundaries.

A great deal of my healing and subsequent courage came as I cultivated healthy boundaries in a therapeutic environment and as I studied the overall topic of boundaries in depth.

As you can tell, I'm very pro-Christian counseling and therapy. But in addition to insight you can glean from a trained professional, there is also a tremendous amount of valuable help available today in books and online resources. Even so, I strongly urge you to measure insight and advice you receive against God's Word to ensure you are not being misled. You will find frequent scriptures and resources referenced throughout these pages, and I encourage you to explore these further in the section at the end of the book.

The Consequences of Change

Once we identify areas in need of change and begin to implement change, we will likely face some resistance in the process, either by our own internal judge or by others who might be more comfortable with how things are. It's imperative to be aware that change brings consequences. Some will be good, others not so much.

In Hebrews 12:1, God compares life on earth to a race. Most of us can relate to that comparison when we take a new course in order to achieve specific changes in life.

Navigating Toward Change

Sometimes, we can clearly see the course ahead of us, the challenging consequences we're going to face. Other times, we have no clue what might be around the corner. The great news is, God knows where we need to go and the twists and turns involved in getting there. He has our race marked out for us. No matter what mile marker we are on, no matter what consequences we might face, He will continue to run alongside us throughout the entire race.

Therefore, we must commit to being intentional in our efforts to run our race faithfully, with perseverance. We must prepare ourselves for battle, from the forces without and from within.

The more we know about how and why we tick, the better able we are to navigate our journey toward change.

The Four Fundamental Foundations of Health

There are four areas of health critical to our well-being. I refer to them as the Four Fundamental Foundations of Health:

1. Spiritual

2. Emotional

3. Relational

4. Physical

These four categories of health are not only critical to the totality of our health, but they profoundly impact one another. Take a look at the Four Fundamental Foundations of Health diagram. Throughout our journey to make fearless choices, we will discuss how each of the 7 Steps to COURAGE impact these four areas of our health.

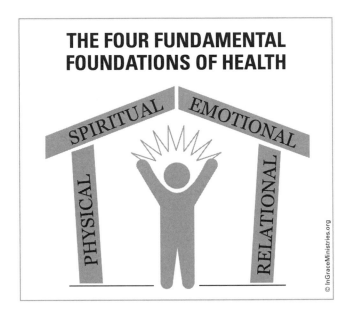

SPIRITUAL HEALTH

When God created humankind, He created us in His image. Just as God exists in three persons—Father, Son, and Holy Spirit—we, too, were created in three parts: body, soul, and spirit.

The apostle Paul clarified this when he said, "Now may the God of peace Himself sanctify you entirely; and may your spirit and soul and body be preserved complete, without blame at the coming of our Lord Jesus Christ."[4]

If we neglect to care for our spiritual health, we neglect a significant aspect of our overall being. It's difficult to dispute that our spiritual health has a profound effect on our emotional, relational, and physical health. Research shows that being spiritually healthy reduces stress, anxiety, and depression. There's no doubt we could spend a great deal of time debating the vast interpretation of *spiritual health*. There are as many definitions of spiritual health as there are religions.

Spiritually healthy people share these traits...

- The ability to receive God's forgiveness and give forgiveness to others.
- The ability to articulate a personal testimony and reflect on a time when Christ became their personal Lord and Savior.
- The ability to recognize God's presence and power in their life.
- The commitment to read and study God's Word while striving to apply accurate biblical truth to life situations.
- The ability to share the gospel and defend the faith.
- The commitment to pray, fellowship, and worship with other believers.
- The commitment to spend time daily with God in prayer and a willingness to listen to His will.

© InGraceMinistries.org

7 STEPS TO COURAGE

When we began our journey together, I gave you full disclosure that my interpretation on living a courageous life is that of a courageous Christian woman. Therefore, I'm going to approach this topic of spiritual health from that perspective.

It is my belief that spiritual health is synonymous with scriptural truth.

God made us from the inside out, and when He changes us, He changes us from the inside out. And I believe the primary way He does that is with His textbook for life, the Holy Bible.

Throughout these pages, I will refer to scriptures pertinent to each step of courage, and we will dig even deeper into the study of God's Word in the *R* step in COURAGE: Replace worldly lies with scriptural truth.

EMOTIONAL HEALTH

People who are emotionally healthy are fully aware of their thoughts, feelings, emotions, and behaviors. They have learned healthy ways to cope with the stress and problems that are a normal part of life.

God created our feelings and emotions as warning signals to tell us when something needs to be examined. These feelings range from mild to intense, positive to negative. And no matter their intensity or type, we must appreciate the insight they provide regarding changes we may need to make.

When we're caught up in running on the gerbil wheel of life, it's common to be guided by what we call "surface emotions" and overlook the deeper, underlying primary emotions at the root of our joy and pain. We will dig much deeper into understanding how to get to the root of our primary feelings in the *U* step in COURAGE: Uncover your true self.

Until then, it's important to be aware that sometimes our emotions can distort our thoughts and lead us to irrational choices. Therefore, we must always

Emotionally healthy people share these traits…

- The ability to recognize, identify, express, and manage feelings.

- The commitment to build and sustain healthy, meaningful relationships.

- The ability to overcome past painful experiences, self-destructive patterns, and distorted beliefs.

- The commitment to be open, truthful, and transparent about needs and feelings.

- The ability to love, respect, and forgive others in spite of differences.

- The commitment to continually self-examine thoughts and actions.

- The ability to face conflict, manage emotions positively, and communicate care in the process.

© InGraceMinistries.org

be proactive in nurturing, protecting, and improving our emotional and mental health. Please refer to chart on page 31.

RELATIONAL HEALTH

God created us to be in relationships with other humans and with Him. While having good spiritual health focuses on our relationship with God, the area of relational health focuses on our relationships with other people in our life.

There are four primary connection levels we experience in human relationships:

1. Common connection

2. Emotional connection

3. Spiritual connection

4. Intimate connection

Throughout life we will experience varying degrees of these connections with different people we come in contact with.

From family to friends to coworkers to acquaintances, relationships come in all shapes and sizes and require love, patience, time, and energy to preserve. Healthy relationships begin with a common connection: common interests, common friends, common hobbies, and the like.

From there we may or may not move forward in our relationship from a common connection to an emotional connection. An emotional connection is a deeper connection with someone we can easily relate to, someone who is easy to be around, and someone we genuinely enjoy spending time with.

Relationally healthy people share these traits...

- The ability to listen non judgmentally to others, value their opinions, and support their goals.

- The commitment to respect others, accept, and take into consideration the feelings, opinions, friends, activities, and interests of others.

- The ability to communicate truth in love to others.

- The commitment to acknowledge, accept responsibility, and ask for forgiveness when wrong.

- The ability to face conflict, recognize resolutions, implement solutions, and communicate with care in the process.

- The ability to love, respect, and forgive others in spite of differences.

- The commitment to be receptive and understanding of others' needs and feelings.

© InGraceMinistries.org

Next we move to the level of a spiritual connection, involving a common harmony in spiritual beliefs. God, out of love and concern for us, speaks to this important component being an integral part of marriage relationships.[5] It is important that we cultivate relationships with people at this level who not only share our common bond of faith but will also encourage and challenge us in our spiritual growth. Please refer to the chart on page 33.

Finally, some relationships reach the level of intimate connection: a closeness that allows each person in the relationship full access to one another's hearts and souls. This type of relationship is commonly seen between parents and children, spouses, close family members, and close friends. Intimate relationships don't always involve physical closeness, but they are always grounded in intimate knowledge of one another, include a sense of safety and security, and are meant to last a lifetime.

Healthy relationships are grounded in the overall health of each person in the relationship, the ability to discern the difference between safe and unsafe relationships, and the ability to set healthy boundaries.

Physical Health

Our physical health can positively or negatively impact all other areas of our foundational health. From improving sleep to preventing chronic disease, everyone can benefit from being more physically fit and active.

There are four basic components of our physical health:

1. Physical activity

2. Nutrition and diet

3. Medical care

4. Rest and relaxation

Physically healthy people share these traits...

- The dedication to daily activity, including leisurely physical activity and structured exercise to maintain strength, flexibility, and endurance.
- The commitment to follow a balanced diet, including proper nutrient intake, fluid intake, and foods for healthy digestion.
- The commitment to abstain from the abusive consumption of drugs and alcohol.
- The dedication to immediately address medical conditions including self-care, major and minor ailments, and injuries.
- The commitment to maintain proper rest and relaxation.
- The commitment to treasure their body as the temple God designed it to be.
- The commitment to drink enough water to maintain proper hydration.

© InGraceMinistries.org

When we neglect proper exercise, eating, medical care, rest, and relaxation, we can weaken our immune systems, develop diseases, and increase our risk of anxiety and depression.

Our blood pressure, energy level, aches and pains, weight loss, and weight gain can be caused by our overall emotional state and, in turn, these physical issues can cause us to experience additional stress and anxiety. And in some cases, damaged emotions can be the driving force that encourages us to abuse substances that can deteriorate and even destroy our overall physical health.

Healthy eating, sufficient rest, and exercise help to reduce our stress, anxiety, and emotional issues. Therefore, it is essential we implement healthy physical practices into our daily lives.

Asking for Help Along the Way

I loved my husband and was prepared to fight for our marriage. But I also knew I would not return home from Israel to make the same choices I always had.

One of the most troubling results of ignoring our struggles is that we become alone in them. Loneliness compounded with hurt is almost always a recipe for despair. My carefully crafted walls of protection and pretending had left me feeling in the dark and completely alone. God convicted me that I had to reach out and ask for help. I had to stop hiding and start seeking.

I felt blessed that my husband was willing to participate in counseling, but I was prepared to go by myself had he not been receptive. Something needed to change, even if that something was only me.

I was ready to change, with or without Mike.

When Mike joined in my resolve to fight for us, we agreed this time the fight would be waged with a professional referee, someone whose experience and objectivity could help us get back on the right track. We couldn't continue the insanity of trying to do that on our own. We were failing miserably at self-diagnosis, and our skills to develop an effective treatment plan weren't any better. We needed someone professional to help us understand and overcome the emotional triggers that seemed to fuel so many of our choices and so many of our arguments.

A good thing about bringing challenging issues into the light is, once you start, the process of uncovering the truth gets easier. It is no coincidence Jesus tells us the truth will set us free, because it does. Truth brings freedom.

But uncovering truth and changing bad habits can sometimes prove to be problematic, especially if we try to do it alone. Additionally, the consequences of change can range from slight to severe, and it's wise to consider objective feedback on the possible outcomes.

Asking for help is one of the hardest steps to take in finding courage to change. Whether it's help from a loved one, friend, pastor, counselor, therapist, or support group, it's a step that can completely alter the course of your life.

With the help of individual counseling, I began to reveal things I had never told anyone before. I also began to realize just how many things I needed to change.

Undergoing any kind of counseling or therapy is hard work. It's like renovating the interior of an old house. You have to first tear down all the damaged and broken walls before you can begin to reconstruct the new infrastructure. And sometimes during the process, you find unexpected problems that need special attention before you can continue. Fortunately, God is a Master Architect, and His blueprint for life is never wrong.

In addition to God's wisdom and grace, we also have trained professionals to help guide us. That's why I've included several charts throughout this book from Robbie Goss.

Robbie is a licensed marriage and family therapist and licensed mental health counselor who runs a thriving private practice in Tampa, Florida. He holds a master of divinity degree from Southwestern Baptist Theological Seminary, an MA in counseling from Liberty University, and in 1990, he established LifeBuilders Christian Counseling Center as a means of linking the local church with professional counseling services. You can read more about Robbie on his website at www.LifeBuildersCounseling.org.

As I navigated the rocky road to understanding real truth and finding courage, I needed to understand why I continued to fall into destructive and dysfunctional patterns. I needed to peel back the many layers of pain and shame that surrounded my heart so I could heal and move on with my life. For me, I knew it was going to take professional counseling to help me better understand myself. This may not be the case for you. Either way, I encourage you to remain open-minded about reaching out for help. Just be certain any professional help you seek comes from a reputable, licensed Christian counselor, therapist, or support group.

As you lean on God for wisdom, guidance, and support, trust Him to lead you to safe people who can love and support you. Trust Him to give you the strength needed to make fearless choices and walk in grace.

COURAGE CALL-TO-ACTION STEPS

1. Take out your notebook or journal and write a page about what healthy boundaries mean to you and how they impact your life.

2. List at least one boundary area you are aware of that you need to change.

3. In your notebook/journal, make four columns and title each column with one of the Four Fundamental Foundations of Health: Spiritual, Emotional, Relational, and Physical. Refer back to the lists that demonstrate each of these areas and take an honest assessment of each category of your health.

4. Write down the health areas you are strongest in, pray for wisdom and discernment, and ask God to tell you how you can strengthen your areas of weakness.

3

C Step in Courage:
Commit to Change

Courage is saying yes to positive challenges.

"Have I not commanded you? Be strong and courageous. Do not be afraid;
do not be discouraged, for the LORD your God will be with you wherever you go."
—*Joshua 1:9, NIV*

*I*t's been said that the hardest part of any unfamiliar journey is the first step. When I returned to the States from Israel, I was prepared to stop repeating my own negative behavior and bring my own issues to light. I was prepared to face the consequences of my choices, whatever they might be.

Once we take this monumental first step, we may find there are more things to change than we anticipated. For example, we may need to change how we view and respond to others in our life, or maybe change our perspective on the situation and circumstances. Perhaps we need to change our attitudes, behaviors, and/or expectations. We may even need to change why we are motivated to change in the first place.

7 STEPS TO COURAGE

Our willingness to identify and commit to specific areas of change will greatly affect our ability to implement change.

There may be many things we need to change on our journey. Everyone's list will be different. For me, I knew one of the first things I needed to change was how I viewed myself. I had an identity crisis that defied all logic. I'd spent so much time trying to ignore myself, I didn't know who I was.

CONVICTED TO CHANGE

The first step in exercising true courage is to be honest with yourself and make the commitment to change the things in life that aren't working. In my case, I had to stop unhealthy habits in order to start making healthy choices. I had to stop living in fantasyland, pretending everything was sunshine and lollipops. I had to stop repeating the same behavior and expecting different results. And I had to stop allowing myself to be in bondage to fear-based choices, whether real or imagined.

Because my own life was such a dysfunctional mess, I developed a clever (and not so unusual) habit. In order not to address my own problems and pain, I spent the majority of my time trying to fix the problems and pain of others.

The Bible addresses this bad habit in no uncertain terms in Matthew: "Why do you stare from without at the very small particle that is in your brother's eye but do not become aware of and consider the beam of timber that is in your own eye?"[1]

No matter how we spin it the fact remains, while we can influence the responses, actions, and reactions of others, we cannot change them. My counselor helped me understand and accept this fact, this bottom line: it's the other person's choice to change (or not), and it's God's job to do the changing (or not).

Commit to Change

Everything changed in Israel when I felt the Spirit of God convict me of the first major courage step I needed to take, the *C* step: Commit to Change, beginning with a commitment to change myself.

I had to stop focusing on how Mike, or other people in my life, needed to change and start focusing on changing the one person I could change: me.

THE ABCs OF CHANGE

There are many areas in life we can proactively change. If we seriously want to commit to change, we need to conduct a soul-searching self inventory and decide what it is we want, or need, to change. So the first question to ask is, "What really needs to change?"

As we strive to strengthen the Four Fundamental Foundations of Health we discussed earlier, there are six key areas of change we must consider as we seek to develop our core strengths:

1. Attitudes

2. Behaviors

3. Beliefs

4. Circumstances

5. Coping skills

6. Desires

Our ability to successfully commit to change is intricately connected to how well we understand the ABCs of what we can change. As you read the brief descriptions of the six areas we have the power to change, grab your notebook and write down the areas that speak strongly to you.

7 STEPS TO COURAGE

Have you ever heard the saying "You need a checkup from the neck up"? Around my house that means someone has a bad attitude that needs to be examined.

Our attitude is our disposition, frame of mind, perspective, temperament, and view. It can also be defined as what we choose to do with our thinking and feelings.

Attitudes range from negative to positive and anywhere in between. One point we are wise to take note of is the effect our attitudes have on our actions and outcomes, which in turn affects our overall fundamental health. A great deal in life hinges on the choices we make concerning our attitudes and actions. These choices stem from events that occur the moment we open our eyes in the morning until we close them at night to sleep.

The Development of a Stronghold chart from Robbie can help us understand the process in which events in our daily lives can eventually lead to strongholds and how our attitudes can be a turning point in this process.

A stronghold is a fortress of thoughts that influences negative attitudes and behaviors.

An event leads to a feeling, which leads to thinking, and then to an attitude. An attitude causes us to act (or react), which can then become a positive or negative habit. A negative habit can become a stronghold.

Let's unpack this further.

When an event happens a *feeling* arises within us. Out of our feeling we develop a particular way of *thinking* about the event. The choices we make regarding our thinking impact the *attitude* we adopt. Therefore, the more control we exercise over our choices, the more control we have over our attitudes.

DEVELOPMENT OF A STRONGHOLD

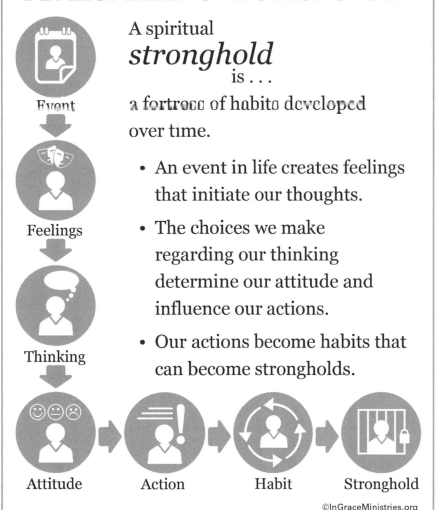

A spiritual

stronghold
is . . .

a fortress of habits developed over time.

- An event in life creates feelings that initiate our thoughts.

- The choices we make regarding our thinking determine our attitude and influence our actions.

- Our actions become habits that can become strongholds.

Event

Feelings

Thinking

Attitude   Action   Habit   Stronghold

©InGraceMinistries.org

But it doesn't stop there. Our attitudes lead to actions, which can become habits and then can become emotional strongholds (something that has control over us). An important point is, in the midst of our attitudes we come face-to-face with choices regarding how we will act. And, of course, for every action there will be a reaction, good or bad. Therefore, if we desire to make healthy, courageous choices, we must commit to changing any of our inappropriate or negative attitudes.

Alas, this sounds a whole lot easier than it is.

Some of my negative attitudes I became aware of were self-pity, self-condemnation, worry, self-righteousness, unforgiveness, and a pattern of negative thinking (such as, the glass is half-empty versus half-full syndrome).

In Philippians the apostle Paul focused on the attitude of believers, urging them to have the same attitude as Christ: one of encouragement, love, affection, and compassion—an unselfish and humble attitude, not only looking out for personal interests but also those of others.[2] Jesus kept a positive perspective and attitude, even when He was mistreated, misunderstood, and mistrusted.

Once I began to realize the effect my attitudes were having on my ability to heal, as well as the effect they were having on my husband, family, friends, and on my overall circumstances, I realized I had to commit to changing them. So I began to turn to God and ask Him to help me adopt healthier attitudes, the attitudes of Christ.

It is important to understand that Satan can put thoughts in our mind, but sin really starts with our attitude, with the choice we make to follow a negative path of thinking rather than to intentionally veer off in a more positive direction.

If we take time to identify and commit to changing our negative attitudes, we will begin to see positive improvements in our actions, habits, strongholds, and relationships.

Commit to Change

There are a host of negative attitudes we adopt that require change in order to move forward toward healthier choices and healthier relationships.

It takes courage to admit we have negative attitudes, and it takes courage to commit to changing them. Read the lists of common Negative versus Positive Attitudes and take an honest inventory of negative attitudes you need to commit to change.

NEGATIVE ATTITUDES VS **POSITIVE ATTITUDES**

NEGATIVE ATTITUDES	POSITIVE ATTITUDES
Angry	Affectionate
Argumentative	Caring
Arrogant	Compassionate
Callous	Considerate
Combative	Encouraging
Envious	Flexible
Hostile	Forgiving
Impolite	Generous
Impractical	Gentle
Indifferent	Giving
Inflexible	Humble
Insensitive	Kind
Insincere	Loving
Pretentious	Patient
Rebellious	Polite
Resentful	Practical
Rude	Sincere
Selfish	Sympathetic
Unforgiving	Understanding
Unsympathetic	Unselfish

© InGraceMinistries.org

BEHAVIOR

Our behavior is the way we act.

There are numerous destructive behaviors we can get trapped in: being pushy, demanding, argumentative, impatient, defensive, critical, or aggressive, just to name a few. We can find ourselves lying, cheating, stealing, isolating, or succumbing to addiction. Poor behaviors have a negative effect on our mind and body as well as on the minds and bodies of those we come in contact with.

Most often there is an underlying problem with handling or expressing our feelings that causes us to act—behave—poorly.

We must take time to identify and manage our negative behaviors because they directly impact our Four Fundamental Foundations of Health: our spiritual, emotional, relational, and physical health.

One way we can begin to identify our negative behaviors is to muster up the courage to ask a trusted friend or loved one to tell us things they recognize we are doing that negatively impact others and ourselves. Sometimes we don't even realize the bad behaviors we are practicing. Other times, we are fully aware of what we are doing, and we realize our actions are inappropriate, but we simply can't stop. We don't know how to stop, and we don't have the courage to reach out and ask for help.

Stopping a bad behavior takes courage; some behaviors take a lot more courage than others. But no matter what, if we are aware of negative behaviors in our lives, now is the time to commit to overcoming those destructive habits and freeing ourselves to live a more joy-filled, productive, and spiritually healthy life.

God's Word clearly tells us that good behavior won't earn us salvation, but believers are urged to practice good behavior as evidence that we have been changed by our salvation.[3]

Remember, thoughts are formed from our feelings, and it's a courageous act to be able to identify our feelings and intentionally choose how we allow them to influence our thoughts, attitudes, and behaviors.

Are there any negative behaviors you are aware of that you need to commit to change?

Review the list below of common negative behaviors and take time to identify these and others you may struggle with. Pray for wisdom and discernment to make the courageous choice to commit to change.

Negative Behaviors

- Abuse
- Aggression
- Arguing
- Bossiness
- Carelessness
- Control
- Deceitfulness
- Manipulation
- Moodiness
- Rudeness
- Spitefulness
- Thoughtlessness

© InGraceMinistries.org

BELIEF

We all have beliefs. Beliefs about life, love, and happiness. Beliefs about what we think matters, why we exist, who we are, and what direction we need to be going.

7 STEPS TO COURAGE

Our belief is our viewpoint or position; it's what we believe to be true about a concept, principle, or idea. If we think about it, it's no small thing: "Lives are routinely sacrificed and saved based simply on what people believe."[4] Beliefs kindle our feelings and emotions about people, places, or things and often cause disputes with others. Our beliefs affect our behaviors, and, therefore, it's critically important we pay attention to them and explore them to determine if they are grounded in logic and truth.

Beliefs are adopted throughout life. We adopt some of our beliefs from parents and caretakers at a young age, and we continue to acquire others through formal education and life experiences.

The important thing to understand about beliefs is they significantly impact our life choices. When difficult or painful events occur, we can develop a distorted belief system based on our pain. As a result, we carry this belief system in our brain as an imprint, and it develops into negative thinking patterns.

God's Word warns us not to believe everything we hear. We must prove or disprove new information before adopting it into our belief system: "Beloved, do not believe every spirit, but test the spirits to see whether they are from God, because many false prophets have gone out into the world."[5]

A significant aspect of being able to walk with courage is to recognize the distorted beliefs (including some downright lies) we've adopted that have created negative thinking patterns that still trigger us today. It's important we learn to reject these lies and replace them with truth. We're going to talk more about this in the *R* step in COURAGE: Replace worldly lies with scriptural truth. However, as we commit to change, it's important to have a basic understanding of the false-belief component.

In my case, there were two consistently negative beliefs that kept me from making fearless choices and walking in courage. These two detrimental lies sucked the lifeblood from my spirit:

Commit to Change

1. I needed the approval of others to be valuable.

2. I needed to care for others and neglect my own God-given needs.

As a result of these negative beliefs, I suffered from tremendous insecurities and expended a great deal of energy trying to please other people in order to gain their approval.

It was a vicious and exhausting cycle.

Remember, there are many distorted beliefs we adopt throughout our life; it's up to us to uncover them and replace them with truth. Are there any distorted beliefs you are aware of that you need to commit to change?

CIRCUMSTANCES

Circumstances are conditions and details that play a role in the outcome of our everyday lives. Our view of our circumstances also plays a significant role in our Four Fundamental Foundations of Health. Circumstances can involve physical, emotional, and situational settings.

Whether we need to change our physical surroundings, implement healthy boundaries, stop enabling behaviors, or start thinking before we react, there are three aspects of our circumstances to consider when committing to change:

1. Some of our circumstances are easier to change than others.

For example, changing our finances, living conditions, or relationships can be more difficult than changing our exercise routine or how we spend our free time.

I am the type who constantly overcommits, and I have a tendency to leave little or no time for relaxing. I had to learn to schedule downtime on my calendar for relaxing in order to get into the habit of fitting relaxation into my day. That was a relatively easy circumstance to change.

As for the circumstances surrounding my relationship with my husband, well that took more time to change and required patience, persistence, and perseverance to see it through.

2. Sometimes it's our perspective of our circumstances that needs to change.

We may feel we are experiencing unfair consequences when in reality they are actually appropriate. Therefore, we must ensure we have an appropriate viewpoint of our circumstances.

When I was in the midst of my marital crisis, there were times I felt as if there was no hope for our relationship; I couldn't see the forest for the trees. In my mind, we were too far gone, too much damage had been done, and nothing could restore the trust that had been broken. But with the help of our counselor my perspective changed, my hope was restored, and I realized, with God's guidance and healing, my heart, our love, and our relationship could be made whole again, and even better than ever.

3. Sometimes it's necessary to involve others in the process of changing our circumstances.

If we are struggling in relationships with others or even in our relationship with ourselves, we may need to involve an objective party to gain clarity on the situation, the circumstance.

For me, I had to learn to come out of isolation and connect with safe people in order to overcome my destructive habits and unhealthy circumstances. We will talk more about this as we discuss overcoming the obstacle of isolation in the next chapter. But it is important to take note of the possibility that we need to include others in our journey to commit to changing our circumstances.

Commit to Change

This is especially important if you are experiencing any kind of physical abuse.

If you find yourself in a physically abusive relationship and fear for your life, it is important that you seek wise counsel regarding any changes you want to make to your circumstances. There are resources within your community, such as safe houses, support groups, and abuse hotlines, that can help you remain safe while changing your emotionally and/or physically dangerous environment. It's important for you to realize you are not alone, and hope and healing is possible.

God gave us our emotions and feelings to help us identify when circumstances in our lives are healthy or unhealthy. It's up to us to pay attention to any warning signals and investigate further in order to determine if change is in order.

Changing unhealthy circumstances in our lives takes courage; some changes take a lot more courage than others. But if we identify circumstances that need to change, check our perspective, involve safe people when necessary, and commit to making a change, we can make courageous choices that will improve our Four Fundamental Foundations of Health.

Are there any unhealthy circumstances in your life you are aware of that need to change? If so, grab your notebook or journal and write down these areas, and then make a commitment today to change them.

COPING SKILLS

Coping skills are simply ways in which we cope, manage, and deal with painful, stressful, and harmful situations in our lives. We adopt both negative and positive coping skills throughout life. Even positive coping skills can be negative if we don't implement them properly. For example, one positive coping skill I employed regularly was physical exercise. It's a well-known fact that physical activity reduces depression and helps us rest better.[6] But exercise can also be a contributor to our problems if we utilize it as an escape from dealing with our issues or if it becomes excessive. The same goes for many other coping strategies. Therefore, even when we incorporate healthy coping mechanisms into our lives, we must remain fully aware of how we are implementing them.

Three detrimental coping skills many of us turn to (myself included) are denial, disassociation, and isolation.

When something is too painful to cope with, we simply tell ourselves, "I'm going to tell myself it didn't really happen," or "I will never tell anyone else it happened." I once knew a woman who always referred to her husband as being "out of town" or "away on business." The reality was, he was in prison and she was in denial. She couldn't cope with the reality of her situation, so she convinced herself everything was okay, a primary example of a destructive coping skill.

I get her mind-set. I spent years wearing masks and convincing myself everything was okay. Sounds crazy, I know, but denial was the way I dealt with painful situations in my life, from as far back as I can remember.

Other times, when life events were too painful to accept, I would choose to disassociate myself from them rather than to simply deny they existed. Even as children, we have the ability to mentally separate ourselves from traumatic events in order to avoid dealing with pain. Post-traumatic stress disorder (PTSD) sufferers often separate themselves from their painful experience, but that numbing separation that once helped them get through the trauma itself eventually gets in the way of their normal development, and they have to heal their separation from the event in order to move on.[7]

For example, for years I experienced reoccurring memories of my dad's anger and verbal threats. Like the time he threatened to tie my brother up and beat him until he bled if he didn't do exactly what he asked him to do. This particular event happened when I was about eight years old, and in order to deal with it and attempt to maintain a relationship with my father, I simply disassociated myself from it. The ugly memory never went away, and I never denied it; I just simply tried to separate myself from it so I could go on with life.

Many of us turn to isolation as a means of coping with fear, shame, and hurt. Rather than reaching out to safe friends and family members when we struggle, we simply retreat into a shell, hide behind internal walls, and convince ourselves we are much better off if no one knows what we're going through.

Implementing healthy coping skills in our lives takes courage. But if we take the time to understand and identify unhealthy ones that need to change and commit to making the necessary changes, we will significantly improve our Four Fundamental Foundations of Health.

What types of coping strategies are you incorporating in your daily life? Are you willing to commit to exchanging negative ones for positive, healthy ones?

It's a courageous action to intentionally address the ABC's of change during a time when we can act rationally and not react emotionally.

Take a look at the lists of common Positive and Negative Coping Skills on the following page and see if you recognize any negative coping skills that you need to commit to changing.

DEFINING OUR DESIRES

Desires can be defined as a powerful craving, longing, or want for something, and they can rule our lives if we allow them to. It's important we have a clear understanding of the difference between our wants and our legitimate needs so we can begin to change how we manage our desires.

NEGATIVE VS POSITIVE COPING SKILLS

NEGATIVE COPING SKILLS

- Isolate
- Abuse substances
- Overeat, shop, or other escape activities
- Mistreat others
- Smoke
- Talk negatively to yourself
- Deny the event happened
- Disassociate yourself from the event
- Act aggressivly or violently toward others
- Work excessively

POSITIVE COPING SKILLS

- Spend quiet time with God
- Exercise by going for a walk, jog, etc.
- Journal thoughts and experiences
- Self-soothe and implement relaxation techniques
- Listen to music
- Seek professional advice
- Talk to a trusted friend
- Set boundaries
- Join a support group
- Write down 10 things you are thankful for

I am thankful for....

© InGraceMinistries.org

Commit to Change

God's Word warns us about being guided by our desires: "Each person is tempted when he is lured and enticed by his own desire. Then desire when it has conceived gives birth to sin, and sin when it is fully grown brings forth death."[8]

While our desires can lead us away from God's will, our legitimate needs can (and should) be met by God and by those we are in a close relationship with. Our need for love, affection, approval, appreciation, attention, encouragement, respect, support, and acceptance are legitimate needs and were given to us by God. We are created with these basic relational needs, yet sometimes we aren't sure how to get them met in healthy ways.

For example, sometimes we *want* love, affection, and validation from another person who isn't willing or capable of giving these things to us. In cases like this, we need to find a healthy solution to meeting these legitimate needs. A healthy solution to this problem would be to first embrace God's love, affection, and approval of us. Second, ask God for guidance to help us get our needs met. And third, seek safe and appropriate relationships to help meet our needs.

Only God promises to meet all of our needs according to His riches in Christ Jesus.[9]

Conversely, it's important we don't get our *needs* and *desires* confused.

Early on, Mike and I had an unhealthy need for each other. Today, we are in a much healthier place, where we don't feel as though we need each other to survive. We now know that only God can fill that role. Instead, we *want* each other.

It feels much better to be wanted rather than simply needed.

Pastor and *Crazy Love* author, Francis Chan, related this concept to our relationship with God when he said, "The irony is that while God doesn't need us but still wants us, we desperately need God but don't really want Him most of the time."[10] Examples of unhealthy desires that can tempt us are power, control, judgment, lust, greed, jealousy, drunkenness, impure acts, sexual immorality, envy, and wild living.

Are there unhealthy desires you struggle with? Are you willing to commit to taking necessary steps to trade in unhealthy desires for healthy ones?

Jesus said, "These things I have spoken to you, so that in Me you may have peace. In the world you have tribulation, but take courage; I have overcome the world."[11]

God knows when we are afraid, and His desire is that we not be afraid but have peace and courage. As children within the family of God, we sometimes need to be reminded to be courageous. We sometimes need encouragement that we are not alone in our circumstances, that we are called to boldly pursue the life God has laid out before us with confidence and in peace.

Therefore, we need to decide now to unpack our emotional baggage. We need to get rid of the negative thoughts, feelings, attitudes, or behaviors that keep us from walking with courage.

It's time to take the *C* step in COURAGE and commit to change.

It's time to find peace.

It's time to find joy in your journey.

The Bible says, "With God all things are possible."[12]

COURAGE CALL-TO-ACTION STEPS

1. Take out your notebook or journal, write down the specific areas within the ABCs of Change you feel led to commit to change. Include additional areas of change God has brought to your attention as you've read this chapter.

2. Pray for wisdom and discernment regarding changes you need to make and write down one positive step you can take in each area of change, whether it involves confrontation, transparency, or seeking help.

3. Share your insights with a trusted friend who will encourage, support, and hold you accountable as you prepare to make the necessary changes.

4. Ask God to help you sincerely commit to change—and not just pretend (see Joshua 1:9; Romans 12:2).

4

O Step in Courage:
Overcome Obstacles

Courage is making wise choices in the face of fear.

*"To him who overcomes, I will grant to eat of the tree of life
which is in the Paradise of God."*
—Revelation 2:7

*M*any of us caught up in the dysfunctional dance of fear-based choices can trace the roots of our distorted thinking back to a time when the baggage we carried was no more than the size of a small tote bag. But those days are long gone, as many of us now carry a matching six-piece set of luggage painfully stuffed with memories of people, places, issues, and things we can never change. We have obstacles on top of obstacles shoved into every compartment.

Some of the baggage we carry is packed with fresh hurt, and some of it we have been lugging around for years. In my experience, there are a great many broken-hearted little girls and boys living inside the shells of broken women and men carrying huge trunkloads of excess baggage.

7 STEPS TO COURAGE

It's time to unpack our bags and lighten the load.

We can do this as we surrender to Christ's call and commit to Him, lessen our burdens, and find rest for our souls.

"Come to Me, all who are weary and heavy-laden, and I will give you rest. Take My yoke upon you and learn from Me, for I am gentle and humble in heart, and you will find rest for your souls. For My yoke is easy and My burden is light."[1]

In this chapter, we're going to identify some of the most common obstacles we need to overcome on our journey to find freedom from bad habits that hold us hostage. As we follow the 7-step process, we will begin to sort through our personal stuff in a more efficient and streamlined manner. We will explore how we got to places of discouragement and fear and then identify what it will take to overcome obstacles and break dysfunctional habits that have consumed our choices for so long.

In our quest for courage, let's think of ourselves like archaeologists who are always committed to digging. It isn't just about one project, one discovery, or one dig. It's about an ongoing commitment to find what's buried underneath the surface of what we can see. Archaeologists have a great many obstacles, like boulders, rocks, sand, trees, and dirt—a lot of dirt—to remove before reaching any kind of treasure. But they're trained to look beyond the surface debris, to look underneath the layers.

When it comes to making fearless choices, we need to train ourselves to look beyond the surface debris—to see past the obstacles in our way and expose the treasures beneath them, like hope, healing, joy, and grace.

Obstacles are often referred to as roadblocks—the hindrances that restrict us from traveling on a clear, unobstructed path. External and internal roadblocks impede our travel, and cause us to be re-routed, detoured, or completely blocked from reaching our destination—achieving our potential.

Overcome Obstacles

Being able to overcome obstacles has been a difficult and oftentimes exhausting experience for me. But I thank God every day for bringing me to a place where I had no choice but to plow through the roadblocks in order to find courage and joy. God allowed me to get to a place of brokenness where I could lay aside many of my fears, and overcome the shame, hurt, and sin that kept me in bondage to fearful choices.

God gave me the strength of a soldier to dig, to remove the surface debris that separated me from the treasures He wanted me to have.

I love what pastor and best-selling author Warren Wiersbe says about overcoming obstacles:

> In the Christian life, you're either an overcomer or you're overcome, a victor or a victim. After all, God didn't save us to make statues out of us and put us on exhibition. He saved us to make soldiers out of us and move us forward by faith to claim our rich inheritance in Jesus Christ.[2]

THE FOUR PESTS OF PRESSURE

While there are often several underlying issues at the root of our obstacles, there are typically four common culprits to blame for many of the problems we face.

Let's review the framework of life, the Four Fundamental Foundations of Health we discussed in an earlier chapter. Think of those four components as the framework of life that make up the walls and roof of our "home." These components comprise our entire life:

1. Spiritual

2. Emotional

3. Relational

4. Physical

Now, think of the Four Pests of Pressure, like invisible termites within the walls of our home, eating away at the framework of our life. We often don't see them, but if left untreated, they will destroy who we are, what we stand for, and why we are here in the first place. Think of these four culprits like parasitic pests feeding on the lifeblood of our existence:

1. Fear

2. Shame

3. Hurt

4. Sin

These Four Pests of Pressure are determined to infiltrate and destroy our lives. And this parasitic infestation isn't a unique problem only a few of us face; we all struggle with them at various times. The problem is, we're often afraid to talk about them, and the less we talk about them the more control they have over us.

When we allow these Four Pests of Pressure to infect our lives, we are left with a weak foundation that is unable to support and protect us throughout the storms of life.

Let's compare the two diagrams showing a healthy foundation versus a foundation that is destroyed by these pesky pests.

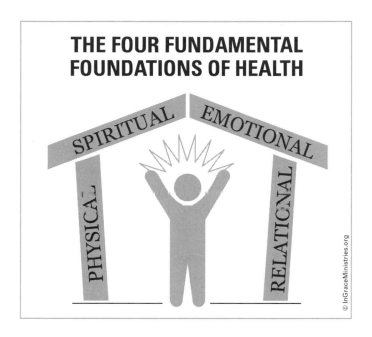

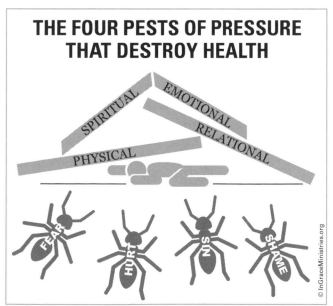

7 STEPS TO COURAGE

Fear

Fear manifests itself in a variety of ways, but it's always working in the background to undermine our emotions. Fear can greatly impact our foundational health.

In a healthy sense, fear functions as an internal alarm system, alerting us when danger is present. But fear can also be the overpowering internal motivator that drives our unhealthy attitudes, behaviors, feelings, desires, and thought patterns.

Several major fears we often experience include:

- Fear of rejection

- Fear of loss

- Fear of abandonment

- Fear of conflict

- Fear of guilt

- Fear of failure

- Fear of exposure

- Fear of embarrassment

- Fear of the unknown

- Fear of being known

Fear can be an all-consuming, powerful emotion that can impact our lives in significant ways.

As I began to dig into my issues of insecurity, codependency, and negative self-talk, it quickly became apparent these problems were fueled by underlying fears, some stemming all the way back to my childhood.

Fear can be the concrete that holds our obstacles together, and it has a profound effect on our ability to be courageous and overcome our obstacles.

The Bible says, "The Lord is my helper, I will not be afraid. What will man do to me?"[3]

SHAME

When I was a little girl, my dad treated me differently than he did my brothers.

Dad would shower me with attention and give me most anything I wanted. He was often kind to me while being overly harsh on my brothers. He spent little time with them, and he often refused to pay for things they needed, like eye exams, glasses, braces, and the like.

This unequal treatment caused me to develop a strong sense of guilt and shame for being who I was. I didn't want to be special if it was at the expense of the brothers I dearly loved.

It was years before I realized that shame had become a significant obstacle in my life.

I didn't suddenly wake up one morning with this epiphany, with the supernatural knowledge this was a key issue in my life and therefore I needed to figure out how to deal with it.

The awareness of the role shame and guilt played in my life came over many years, through countless hours of counseling, reading, experiencing, and observing.

Author Brené Brown, who specializes in the research of shame and vulnerability, said, "Shame is an intensely painful feeling or experience of believing that we are flawed and therefore, unworthy of love and belonging."[4]

Wow.

Until I read those words, I didn't realize how much I needed to exterminate this pest that sabotaged my life and stole my joy.

The authors whose work I often quote were instrumental in my growth. We are blessed to live in an age where an abundance of valuable information is available at our fingertips. On the other hand, there is also an abundance of, shall we say, nonsense, so be careful whose advice you take.

For example, when I read this following paragraph from *Daring Greatly*, I was profoundly impacted on my walk of courage:

> People trapped by shame hide behind ego defensives, masks, negative behaviors, and addictions. A person has to realize their problems are related to a deeper issue of how they look at themselves. If we only address our outward problems, we address only the symptoms rather than addressing the real issue. Overcoming shame means to get in touch with where shame started in our lives. The four main sources of shame are: sin, abandonment, abuse, and traumatic events. Understanding shame is critical to overcoming it.[5]

HURT

We've all experienced hurt at one time or another, but the impact it has on our life after the experience is often more significant than the actual hurt itself.

If we allow it to, hurt becomes a pattern we get stuck in. We relive our hurt over and over again in our minds, and it chips away at the very foundation of our spiritual, emotional, relational, and physical health.

Therefore, past hurts must be uncovered and dealt with so we will be free to step out in courage, overcome obstacles, and move on with our lives.

Overcome Obstacles

When Mike and I started counseling, neither of us had a clue that many of our behaviors were a direct result of childhood hurts. Like many successful adults, we gave little credence to events that occurred so long ago.

We lived by the creed "That was then and this is now," and we diminished the fundamental and foundational power our early experiences carried.

We both ignored the damaged little children still being held captive by painful memories and heartfelt hurt.

As a young girl, I longed for a relationship with my brothers, but to have that I would need to sacrifice the relationship with my father. It was a no win situation in my eyes. I felt disconnected from honest, loving relationships. I learned the only way to get my emotional needs met was to cling to unhealthy relationships and ultimately live for the approval others.

And the only way to get approval from others was to be who I thought they wanted or needed me to be, not who I really was.

Sin

Sin is sneaky; it's always lurking in the background, waiting for just the right moment to influence our decisions, desires, behaviors, actions, and relationships. Sin is one of the most deceptive and powerful destroyers we face.

We are exposed to three types of sin each and every day:

1. Sin against us

2. Sin in the world

3. Sin by us

Matthew speaks clearly to each of these temptations in God's Word.

Sin Against Us: "Whoever causes one of these little ones who believe in Me to stumble, it would be better for him to have a heavy millstone hung around his neck, and to be drowned in the depth of the sea" (Matthew 18:6).

Sin in the World: "Woe to the world because of its stumbling blocks! For it is inevitable that stumbling blocks come; but woe to that man through whom the stumbling block comes!" (Matthew 18:7).

Sin by Us: "If your hand or your foot causes you to stumble, cut it off and throw it from you; it is better for you to enter life crippled or lame, than to have two hands or two feet and be cast into the eternal fire" (Matthew 18:8).

Sin targets the desires of the flesh. Desires that, at their root are legitimate, yet when not met in ways God intended, the result will always be regret, pain, and destruction.

Satan, the father of sin, desires nothing more than to steal, kill, and destroy our foundational health with his lies and deception. If we stick our head in the sand and ignore the reality of temptation and sin, we will find it very hard, if not impossible, to overcome obstacles in our lives.

We will tackle this topic further in the *A* step in COURAGE: Accept the things you cannot change. But for now, let's understand and be on guard against the role sin plays in the destruction of our health and in the inability to overcome obstacles.

COMMON OBSTACLES

It's impossible to list the full range of obstacles that can cause roadblocks in our life. Consider the list below as our Top Ten Common Obstacles, and know you are not alone if you can relate to experiencing any of these in your life.

Overcome Obstacles

Remember, many of these obstacles can be directly connected to one or more of the Four Pests of Pressure. When we can identify and address the pressure, we can more readily address the obstacle and overcome it.

TOP TEN COMMON OBSTACLES

1. Relational conflict

2. Codependency

3. Triggers/landmines

4. Expectations

5. Anger

6. Isolation/secrecy

7. Anxiety/stress

8. Bitterness/unforgiveness

9. Addictions

10. Abuse

RELATIONAL CONFLICT

Relational conflict occurs when individuals experience incompatibility with one another regarding their needs, goals, or roles.[6] Often we choose to avoid rather than to confront a difficult person or situation. We tend to rationalize our decision to do nothing by saying things like, "I don't need to get involved. What difference would it make anyway?" or, "It would be better for me to simply find a way to live with this situation rather than to muster up the courage to confront it."

All conflict, whether it's within a marital relationship or any other relationship, requires that both parties communicate with care and work to understand each other's individual positions. Careful communication is the key to finding middle ground so both parties can move forward in the relationship.

When approaching conflict directly, it's important to take a close look at our own contribution to the problem. After we have considered our role in the conflict, we need to prepare to resolve the issues for which we are responsible. We do this by asking for forgiveness from the other person, if necessary, and discussing the conflict openly while showing care and respect for the other person.

For me, there have been many times I would find myself in the midst of conflict because I had not implemented appropriate boundaries, I was expecting too much, or I was focused on having to be right rather than trying to see the other person's point of view. What I needed to do was take a step back and consider my contribution to the conflict. Then, with prayer and preparation, I had to show care for the other person, all the while speaking truth in love.

Conflict, while easier for some to manage than others, is never easy. But, that's no excuse to avoid it. We must work to improve our ability to manage relational conflicts in grace-filled ways so our strained relationships might be healed.

Codependency

Author Melody Beattie explains the definition of a codependent as "one who has let another person's behavior affect him or her and who is obsessed with controlling that person's behavior, whether it is a child, spouse, loved one, friend, or client." [7] In the same book, author Ernie Larson defines codependency as "self-defeating, learned behaviors that result in a diminished capacity to initiate or participate in loving relationships."[8]

Overcome Obstacles

In other words, codependency is an unhealthy attachment to another person, an overwhelming feeling that we can't be complete, whole, or valuable if we don't take care of, fix, or meet the needs of the other person we are attached to.

My mother modeled codependency beautifully for me. She and I were close; I considered her my best friend. I saw my mother as a strong woman, someone who could endure disappointments, difficulties, and even abuse. She was beautiful, honest, a realist, and someone who could persevere in the most difficult of circumstances. It wasn't until I began to work with my counselor that I began to realize my mom's apparent strength, outlook, and perseverance were actually covering up her underlying pain, disappointment, and fear.

Codependency is not something we choose. It is a legitimate issue that finds its origin in past trauma or fear, and most often is a result of being in relationships with emotionally unhealthy people.

Codependency is like a disease: left untreated it can spread throughout your life like cancer. Yet unlike cancer, a disease that only consumes the individual who has it, codependency spreads to those you are in relationship with. It can be handed down to your children and can foster the issues and struggles of loved ones.

For me, ignoring its existence would have been an emotional death sentence. I had to overcome this obstacle or drown in my dysfunction. At my breaking point, learning this term helped me better understand my struggles and take the necessary steps toward managing them. The process proved to be a marathon, though, rather than a jog through the park.

For codependents, it is critically important for our emotional health not to underestimate the power and control codependency has on our lives. Left untreated, stuffed, denied, or underestimated, codependency will continue to grow and maintain its control over our life until we finally reach the point where the pain of staying the same becomes greater than the pain of making the change.

A large part of overcoming codependency is realizing how we view ourselves. Those of us with codependent characteristics must recapture our ability to authentically feel the entire spectrum of our own true feelings and learn to talk about them with safe people, such as a counselor, support group, sponsor, or mentor. Celebrate Recovery is a wonderful support group offering valuable insight into self-discovery.

TRIGGERS AND LANDMINES

Emotional triggers are issues, actions, and events that can set off a flashback of a painful memory, which in turn provokes negative responses. When we experience a flashback, our response to our current situation is generally intensified and can sometimes be blown entirely out of proportion.

Landmines, on the other hand, are emotional triggers that are especially sensitive and/or painful that can cause us to overreact, melt down, blow up, and cause serious damage to relationships.

For example, when Mike would raise his voice toward our children and attempt to discipline them, I would often intervene because it triggered memories of my dad's anger. At the same time, Mike would be triggered by my interference because it triggered his memories of disrespect and disregard by his dad. This set off a series of unhealthy, emotionally reactive choices on both our parts.

Repeated often, these particular triggers grew into landmines and resulted in consequences that would last weeks, even months. Mike and I would fall into a cycle of withdrawal and silent treatment accompanied by jabs of criticism and sarcasm, which only added to the deterioration of our relationship. It was a vicious and destructive cycle.

Overcome Obstacles

Learning to identify our triggers and landmines helped Mike and me realize areas of fear, shame, hurt, and sin that needed healing. Once we began to deal with these Four Pests of Pressure that fueled our triggers, we gained understanding and more control of our own responses and became more compassionate toward each other. We learned how to act rationally and intentionally instead of reacting emotionally. As a result, we've grown in our ability to walk in God's grace.

EXPECTATIONS

Every feeling has an expectation attached to it. For example, when I was angry with Mike because of negative comments or sarcasm, I had an expectation that he was supposed to always be kind and never say mean things to me. Although this would be nice, my expectations were unrealistic. Mike is a good man and never set out to intentionally hurt me, but he had his own inner demons to deal with. My unrealistic expectations were certainly not the cause of our increasing marital problems, but they were an obstacle in my ability to walk with courage and conviction.

We can exhaust ourselves by expecting others to respond to situations the same way we would. Have you ever said, "I can't believe she did that! I would never even *think* of doing something like that!" The truth is, we live in a world where people don't always share or live up to our expectations, and sometimes this reality hurts us.

The joy of diversity is a blessing, but our differences can bring some of the most complicated challenges to the surface. Having different personality types, opinions, choices, and expectations is natural.

When we have an unrealistic expectation, the only positive way to handle it is to give it to God and then let it go. On the other hand, if our expectation is realistic, we need to speak the truth in a caring way, at the right time, to the person we are communicating with.

The key in this equation is to know what is realistic versus unrealistic.

This takes prayer, introspection, and sometimes professional help.

In the situation with Mike, I had an unmet need for respect in all situations and circumstances, not just in times of our disagreement. But the Bible does not say it is our spouse's responsibility to supply all of our needs all of the time. It does say, however, that God desires to supply all of our needs all of the time. Therefore, at times when my spouse wasn't in a position to provide it, I needed to ask God to meet my need for respect and to give me the ability to be respectful at the same time.

Sometimes, God meets our needs directly, while at other times He meets our needs through relationships with others.

Anger

Scripture says, "Be angry, and yet do not sin; do not let the sun go down on your anger, and do not give the devil an opportunity."9

Anger is an intense emotional reaction to a painful, disappointing, or devastating event in life. It is a legitimate feeling that, when experienced, must be dealt with, otherwise it adversely affects our physical and emotional health as well as the health of our relationships.

As Mike and I journeyed through counseling, I began to experience a lot of anger, anger I didn't really have a clue how to manage at first. When we experience anger, we typically deal with it in one of two ways: we externally act out or we internally allow it to build up.

I spent many years stuffing hurts and unmet expectations. They intensified like a volcano building pressure and caused me to act out in anger when they finally erupted.

Overcome Obstacles

In counseling, I realized some of the hurts that took place in my early life were actually contributing to the anger I was directing toward Mike. I had never dealt with feeling unloved, disrespected, not valued, and not cherished.

Overcoming the obstacle of anger requires us to get in touch with our underlying feelings, realize our relational needs, and face our unmet expectations. It means we need to know who we really are underneath all our surface feelings of anger. We'll talk more about this in the *U* step in COURAGE as we unpack what it means to uncover your true self.

ISOLATION AND SECRECY

The Bible says, "Whoever isolates himself seeks his own desire; he breaks out against all sound judgment."[10]

Isolation and secrecy cripple our ability to heal. It's a common behavior we develop in order to deal with the Four Pests of Pressure: fear, shame, hurt, and sin. It's vital we let these obstacles go and learn to connect on a deeper level with safe people. Isolation tricks us into believing three dangerous lies:

1. It is safe here.

2. This is good for me.

3. I can't trust anyone.

Throughout the early years of our marriage, I mastered the art of isolation and secrecy. As our relationship struggled, I attempted to busy my life with activities involving my kids, family, friends, and church. I worked hard to hide everything from everyone who knew us. I didn't want to burden anyone with my problems, I didn't want to chance being judged, and I couldn't allow people to get too close, otherwise they might see behind my carefully crafted mask. I didn't understand that isolating myself was actually contributing to the problem rather than helping it.

7 STEPS TO COURAGE

God gave me supernatural courage to come out of isolation that night in Israel when I felt lost, alone, helpless, and covered in a cloak of deep sadness and secret shame.

Even though it was difficult, the choice to come out of hiding put me on a path to uncovering secrets—some I had kept buried for more than thirty years.

My walls of isolation began to break down quickly when I took the courageous step to come out of isolation and invite safe friends into my situation.

One of the first steps to overcoming isolation is to identify a safe person to share your struggles with. Mike and I were blessed. The first two people we uncovered our issues with were willing to love us unconditionally, regardless of the amount of ugliness that needed to be unearthed from our past.

As I began to embrace transparency and honesty around others, God convicted my spirit that He didn't want me to stop with just one safe friend. He knew I needed to enlist other safe friends who would love me unconditionally and help me realize I wasn't alone in what I was going through. My counselor gave me the assignment of building what he called a life team. A team of safe friends I could be completely transparent around who could nonjudgmentally handle my junk. I could also trust this team to love me in the midst of my healing. We all need friends who will listen attentively, love us unconditionally, pray accordingly, and speak truth boldly! Satan, on the other hand, desires to keep us from close relationships with godly people. One of his key strategies is to keep us in isolation and secrecy. Don't give him that power!

Remember, two are better than one,[11] and God's Word encourages us to be in healthy relationships that can build us up, encourage us, and help us when our burdens are too much to bear.

Overcome Obstacles

ANXIETY AND STRESS

Anxiety and stress are generally birthed out of fear, shame, hurt, and sin. We may be stressed at work, anxious over an upcoming event or any number of issues, but until we identify the underlying Four Pest of Pressure fueling our stress and anxiety, we will continue to suffer. Stress and anxiety are two common emotions, and both can have a detrimental effect on all four components of our foundational health.

I remember the first time I was asked to speak in front of a small group of people. I was so anxious I was sweating, and I found it hard to breathe. With God's help, I managed to get through this experience. Little did I know, speaking was a gift God was uncovering in my life in order to prepare me for full-time ministry. Just like fear, a healthy dose of anxiety can be good. When we are a little anxious about an upcoming event, experience, or project, we are more likely to prepare for it. But when our anxiety becomes an obstacle causing us to have health issues, relational issues, or to turn down opportunities to share our story with others, we would be wise to take the necessary steps to overcome it.

God's Word tells us, "Do not be anxious about anything, but in every situation, by prayer and petition, with thanksgiving, present your requests to God." [12]

We can overcome anxiety and stress when we learn to trust God and give Him control over our life.

Not long after speaking to that first small group, close friends asked me to speak at the funeral of their sixteen-year-old daughter, who was tragically killed in a plane crash a few weeks before Christmas. My first thought was, *How in the world can I do this?* But I quickly listened to the Holy Spirit's voice of encouragement as it reminded me to "seek the LORD and His strength." [13]

I knew without a doubt I didn't have the confidence, strength, or ability on my own to maintain my composure to speak at such an emotional event, especially since I was so close to this family and to their daughter. The only way I could do it was to trust God to give me the strength and the words to say. I had less than twenty-four hours to prepare.

Less than an hour before the funeral, my friends gave me a letter they wrote the night before—a good-bye letter to their daughter they wanted me to read.

Dear Lord, how can I do this?

On the way to the funeral, I started reading out loud and barely got through the first page before I was crying and couldn't go on. I refolded the letter and began to pray.

Lord, I need Your supernatural strength to do this!

God didn't let me down.

More than six hundred people attended the funeral, and I am eternally grateful I trusted God to help me face my fear and anxiety so I could participate in honoring this special family and their very special daughter.

If anxiety and stress have become obstacles in your life, if they are causing you to lose sleep, turn down opportunities, or overeat (or go without food), perhaps it's time to commit to change and take the necessary steps to overcome these destructive obstacles.

BITTERNESS AND UNFORGIVENESS

The apostle Paul said, "Let all bitterness and wrath and anger and clamor and slander be put away from you, along with all malice. Be kind to one another, tender-hearted, forgiving each other, just as God in Christ also has forgiven you." [14]

Bitterness often results when we have an unresolved conflict. An emotion often found at the root of bitterness is unforgiveness. When we allow conflict and issues within relationships to fester, rather than dealing with them up front, we open the door to unforgiveness that in turn can eventually become bitterness. Whether we need to forgive others or ourselves, until we fully forgive, we will be unable to completely dismantle other barriers in our life. I've heard it said that unforgiveness is like drinking poison and waiting for the other person to die.

Bitterness affects us in devastating ways: spiritually, emotionally, relationally, and physically. Once the bondage of bitterness is broken, it frees us to rebuild our fundamental foundations of health.

Bitterness is related to feelings of hurt that have been repressed or ignored. In order to overcome it, we have to admit we were hurt by someone and learn how to heal that hurt.

"See to it that no one comes short of the grace of God; that no root of bitterness springing up causes trouble, and by it many be defiled." [15]

I realized I had developed bitterness toward my dad regarding how he treated my brothers, my mom, and me. In counseling, I learned how to embrace grace to heal from that pain and forgive my father.

We need to embrace God's grace in order to heal and forgive.

Addictions

"Addictions," says Joseph Frascella, director of clinical neuroscience at the National Institute on Drug Abuse, "are repetitive behaviors in the face of negative consequences, the desire to continue something you know is bad for you." [16]

Addictions can be behavioral or chemical. From gambling to shopping to alcohol, drugs, or sex, they often start out as habits that slide into addictions. The two principal characteristics of addiction are denial and projection. Denial says, "I don't have a problem," and projection says, "You or someone else is my problem." The biggest challenge in working with people who have addictions is getting them to address these two characteristics.

Addictions open the floodgates to the pleasure center of the brain. They become much more enticing when an individual has experienced a lot of intense trial and tribulation. The addiction becomes a compulsive escape from the pain. In order to overcome addictions, it is important to realize they are a stronghold that must be torn down one step at a time.

Some addicts will require inpatient treatment if they are addicted to a chemical. According to researchers at Yale University, ninety days seems to be an average period of time for the brain to correct the decision-making and thinking functions.[17]

Programs that focus on getting the addict to initially stop drinking or drugging usually last about thirty days. Programs focused on helping the addict to change thinking patterns usually last ninety days. The most effective programs, however, seem to focus on lifestyle rebuilding and generally last from six months to a year. There are several Christian programs of this type that have proven to be successful. Conducting an Internet search will yield many options. Be sure to take the time to conduct thorough research on available programs and contact references. And always remember, although we can conduct interventions for addicted loved ones and provide them with resources and encouragement, it's the addict who must be ready to overcome this obstacle, not someone else who tells them it's time to do so.

The following resources are good places to seek help:

The American Association of Christian Counselors
www.AACC.net

Overcome Obstacles

Celebrate Recovery
www.CelebrateRecovery.com

Narcotics Anonymous
www.NA.org

Alcoholics Anonymous
www.AA.org

Abuse

A friend of mine was sharing about an issue with a family member. For years, the family member had cursed, belittled, and falsely accused her. After listening to her story, I asked, "Why do you allow this person to verbally abuse you? You do understand that you can make a choice to put a healthy boundary in place with this person, right?"

It was like a light bulb was suddenly turned on for my friend.

She didn't realize she was tolerating verbal abuse until it was gently and lovingly pointed out to her. Her situation reminded me of the story of a scientist who conducted an experiment with a frog.

A scientist put a frog into a pan of hot water. The frog jumped out. Then she put a second frog into a pan of cool water. This frog didn't jump out. Slowly, the scientist raised the temperature of the water, and the frog gradually adapted until it boiled to death.

My friend had gradually adapted to her pan of hot water. She didn't realize how bad the abuse had become, but it was killing her spirit.

Abuse can be verbal, emotional, physical, or sexual.

Verbal abuse involves threats, insults, humiliation, blaming, yelling, and intimidation. Emotional abuse can take many different forms, such as depriving someone of care, playing mind games, humiliating or bullying someone directly or indirectly, using threats of violence toward others in order to control them, and controlling through intimidation. Physical abuse can take several forms, as well, including slapping or punching, pushing and shoving, destroying property, using a weapon to control or intimidate, or restraining someone against their will. Sexual abuse includes any sex that is nonconsensual, even if it's between a husband and wife.

Malachi 2:16 is often quoted to encourage abuse victims to stay in abusive marriages, yet many people leave off the second half of this verse that says God not only hates divorce, but He also hates a man who mistreats his wife: "'For I hate divorce,'" says the LORD, the God of Israel, "'and him who covers his garment with wrong and violence,'" says the LORD of hosts. "'Therefore keep watch on your spirit, so that you do not deal treacherously [with your wife].'"[18]

Abuse of any type is destructive to the victim and to children of any age who are exposed to the abuse. Therefore, abuse should be dealt with promptly and approached with care and caution.

The information in this book is not in any way intended to constitute professional advice or serve as a recommendation to take a particular course of action. As I mentioned previously, there are resources within your community, such as safe houses, support groups, and abuse hotlines that can help you make informed decisions about your circumstances.

If you or someone you know is experiencing any symptoms of abuse, seek wise counsel immediately. When necessary, do not hesitate to call the authorities, particularly when a vulnerable underage child is involved.

Let's take a look at the following list of components of a healthy relationship versus an abusive relationship.

HEALTHY RELATIONSHIP VS ABUSIVE RELATIONSHIP

HEALTHY RELATIONSHIP	ABUSIVE RELATIONSHIP
Acceptance	Blame
Affirmation	Condescension
Comfort	Control
Compromise	Criticism
Connection	Degradation
Forgiveness	Hitting
Freedom	Humiliation
Honesty	Insults
Humility	Intimidation
Partnership	Isolation
Respect	Lies
Responsibility	Minimizing
Safety	Nagging
Satisfaction	Name Calling
Solutions	Neglect
Support	Property Destruction
Togetherness	Slander
Trust	Stalking
Understanding	Threats
Validation	Violence

© InGraceMinistries.org

Overcoming Obstacles

If you are struggling with any of these or other issues and are ready to commit to change and overcome obstacles, there's no better time than right now to begin. Instead of emotionally reacting to these obstacles when they appear, seek professional counseling, support groups, sponsors, or mentoring programs that can help you work through the fear, shame, hurt, and sin that fuels any negative or counterproductive behavior. Decide now how you will intentionally act to address these issues.

Being able to identify the obstacles is a significant component in your ability to implement a practical plan to overcome them.

COURAGE CALL-TO-ACTION STEPS

1. Spend quiet time with God. Pray for wisdom and discernment to recognize the obstacles that hinder your foundational health. Listen attentively to God and ask Him for guidance to overcome your obstacles.

2. Take out your notebook or journal and write down the obstacles you need to overcome.

3. Beside each obstacle, write down which of the Four Pests of Pressure are contributing to your obstacles: fear, shame, hurt, sin. There may be more than one of these culprits fueling each obstacle.

4. Reach out to a safe person, admit your obstacles, and ask for support as you work through the process of overcoming them. Don't wait. Get help.

5

U Step in Courage: Uncover Your True Self

Courage is being honest with others and ourselves.

"The Spirit you received does not make you slaves, so that you live in fear again; the Spirit you received brought about your adoption to sonship."
—Romans 8:15 NIV

What we believe about ourselves affects our ability to make courageous choices.

It's critical to take an up-close and personal look at how we view ourselves. Being able to experience the amazing transformation that comes from seeing ourselves through God's eyes is life changing. When we embrace our identity in Christ and learn to love ourselves in healthy ways, it frees us to treasure and love others in healthy ways.

Like most little girls growing up, I wanted to be accepted by my peers. So I didn't dare let any of my friends know about the time my dad threatened to tie my brother up and beat him until he bled, or when dad reached across the table at dinner to physically shut me up for saying something he didn't like.

I believed I couldn't share any of that, so when I went to school or hung out with friends, I put on a happy face and became the person I thought they would want to hang around with.

Have you ever felt the need to hide who you really are?

Not only did I need to be accepted by friends, but from as far back as I can remember, I wanted and needed the attention I got from boys. My identity was tied up in my relationships with the opposite sex. As a result of not having a stable relationship with my dad and having broken parents as an example, I developed an unhealthy view of what relationships between boys and girls should look like.

In my mind, a loving relationship with the opposite sex was based on my ability to please that other person, no matter how it made me feel. In the big-picture equation, how I felt wasn't important. There was an emotionally damaged Ann inside me whose distorted thoughts controlled my actions, and she said things like, *Just keep everyone in your life happy because if you don't, they might get angry or reject you.*

Have you ever been so fearful of losing someone's love or attention that you find yourself doing things you really don't want to do, just to keep them from rejecting you? To me, rejection was like being stabbed in the heart, and I had to do whatever it took to keep from experiencing it.

When Mike voiced disapproval of how much time I was spending at church, I tried once again to be what I thought he wanted me to be, and, terrified of rejection, I put my relationship with God into a carefully crafted box.

I thought I could make it work. All I had to do was figure out how I could learn more about God and get closer to Him, while at the same time pleasing Mike by not doing either of those things on the weekends when he wanted our family to be together.

I was nothing if not accommodating.

Uncover Your True Self

When I didn't have enough courage to "obey God rather than men,"[1] God didn't give up on me. He continued to work with me. He directed my path toward a resolution that helped me move forward until I gained courage.

That's when a friend told me about Precept Ministries, and I drove forty-five minutes to Chattanooga to attend one of their women's conferences. Author and ministry founder, Kay Arthur, is a woman God has used in mighty ways to encourage and empower believers.

It was at this event I learned about their weekly pilot Bible studies, and I immediately saw this as the answer to my dilemma. I could attend classes on Tuesdays while Mike was at work and learn to study God's Word without disrupting the flow of our life.

The thing is, the more I studied, the hungrier I got. Once God's Word really takes hold of your heart, it's hard to contain the passion. He doesn't want to be contained and controlled. He doesn't want us to live a double-standard life.

What I didn't know at the time was this was all part of God's desire to draw me closer to Him. There are no accidents in God's kingdom. He has a plan and purpose for each of our lives.

Could it be you are reading this today as part of God's plan? As an answer to prayer? God wants you to be courageous. And He wants you to embrace His love and grace and experience the abundant life He makes available to each and every one of us.

A CHILD OF GOD

God didn't want me to put my growing relationship with Him in a box. He wanted me to get to a place where an honest and loving relationship with Him would take precedence in my life and become the central hub of my heart. He wanted me to completely grasp the depth of His love for me (the *G* step in

COURAGE), something I was unable to do until I uncovered my true self and understood my identity in Christ—my birthright as a daughter of the King.

It's good to take an honest, unvarnished look at what we are going to change in order to make fearless choices—overcoming the obstacles that hinder our forward movement, for example. But it's equally important to take the same honest and unvarnished look inside at whom we are going to change as we learn to walk with courage.

It's written in the proverb, "As water reflects the face, so one's life reflects the heart." [2]

Being able to uncover our true self begins in our heart. It's about embracing our God-given value and reflecting our true identity as a child of God. It's about knowing who—and *whose*—we are: "Search me, O God, and know my heart; try me and know my anxious thoughts; and see if there be any hurtful way in me, and lead me in the everlasting way." [3]

For years, my identity was dependent on how others viewed me, and I learned early to cover up areas of my life I believed were unbecoming or unacceptable. I started to wear masks as a young girl. By the time I was an adult, I couldn't tell the difference between who I really was and who I wanted others to see. In essence, I had become invisible.

There is power in being invisible—if you are a superhero.

Otherwise, it's a lonely place to be.

In counseling, a common statement heard by therapists is, "I don't know who I am." In other words, "The real me is invisible; I have lost my identity."

At one time or another, some of us try to hide who we really are. If we're being honest, many of us have believed if friends and loved ones really knew us, they wouldn't—couldn't—fully accept us. And so, we often go to painstaking efforts to show the world around us we can beautifully masquerade as the person we think they want us to be.

Uncover Your True Self

The problem with hiding behind masks is, we never get to exhibit who we really are, and, as a result, we are often left with feelings of deceit, guilt, and aloneness. In many cases we lose touch with our true self. We lose our sense of identity.

When we talk about identity, we are referring to how we see ourselves—to our awareness of our personal uniqueness. It's a lack of this awareness that causes an identity crisis.

When we don't have a clear, consistent sense of who we are, we often allow others to define it for us. And when we don't have a sense of *whose* we are, we can often devalue our self-worth. Together, this is a lethal combination.

If we have spent any length of time making fear-based choices, there is a strong chance we may have neglected to develop our true identity as a person. But our true self is still there, somewhere, and it's never too late to find this unique child of God.

FINDING OUR TRUE SELF

The reasons we are hesitant (or afraid) to reveal our true identity or true feelings to others are as varied as our DNA. My issues were different from those of my parents and are most likely different from yours. However, the common denominator in any scenario of learning how to make courageous choices is that we must stop hiding and start seeking. Never is that more true than when it comes to finding out who we are.

I learned the art of hiding, or covering up, as a little girl from a mother who never shared her true self with anyone. She was the wife of a man who often mistreated her and the mother of children often being mistreated by the same man. Today, my heart breaks when I think of how hard it must have been for her to maintain that stoic mask of pretense, a mask I learned to model early in life.

7 STEPS TO COURAGE

As I grew up, I kept thinking if I did what I was supposed to do, if I protected myself and others from being unfairly judged, and if I waited patiently and pretended long enough, things would somehow get better.

I existed for years in this dysfunctional delusion.

In covering, hiding, and pretending, I completely bought into the worldly lie that I couldn't share my pain or confusion with anyone.

In fact, I continued to cover up fear, shame, hurt, sin, and a suitcase full of distorted beliefs for years—even after becoming an avid student of God's Word and even for several years after I began teaching the Bible to others.

While I don't discount how God has used the painful experiences in my life, I can't deny that I often look back in regret on the wasted years, the years I existed in a fog of invisible identity. God's Word says, "He who covers his sins will not prosper, but whoever confesses and forsakes them will have mercy." [4] It was years before I embraced the reality of this truth. Years of making fearful choices based on a false belief system that shattered my sense of self-worth. Years that I pray I can help you avoid as we take these courageous steps together.

THE CORE OF OUR IDENTITY: WHO WE ARE, WHOSE WE ARE

Satan would like nothing more than to keep us from truly embracing whose we really are.

When I was first saved I was clueless about who God was, how He defined me, and how much He deeply loved me. I embraced the beliefs that I would go to heaven and my sins were forgiven, but I couldn't grasp much more than that. I had no idea what it meant to be a new creation in Christ, so I kept lugging around my trunk of fear, shame, hurt, and sin as if it would always be a permanent fixture in my life. This habit lasted for almost three decades until I finally learned how to unpack my emotional baggage and embrace what God thought of me.

The Bible says, "Therefore if anyone is in Christ, he is a new creature; the old things passed away; behold, new things have come." [5]

God knows who we are, where we are, and what we are, and He loves us unconditionally right in the midst of it all. As believers, we must embrace the fact that our past doesn't define us, our success or failure doesn't define us, the opinions of others don't define us, what we have or don't have doesn't define us, and our fear, shame, hurt, and sin don't define us—God does.

It is God—and only God—who defines us.

"By this the love of God was manifested in us, that God has sent His only begotten Son into the world so that we might live through Him." [6] We must cast out any belief about ourselves that isn't from God, and reject what others say about us that isn't coming from a genuine place of truth and love.

We must believe what God's Word says about us. In His eyes we are all these:

- Fearfully and wonderfully made (Psalm 139:14)
- Designed by God (Ephesians 2:10)
- Created in the image of God (Genesis 1:27)
- Bought with the ultimate price, the blood of Christ (1 Corinthians 6:20)
- A new creation in Christ (2 Corinthians 5:17)
- Recipients of God's grace through Christ (Romans 5:2; Ephesians 1:6)
- Conquerors through Christ (Romans 8:37)
- Blessed with spiritual blessings in Christ (Ephesians 1:3)
- Sealed in Christ for the day of redemption (Ephesians 1:13; 4:30)
- Justified, saved, and at peace with God through Christ (Romans 5:1–9)

7 STEPS TO COURAGE

As children of God, we are to walk in a manner worthy of our calling (Ephesians 4:1–3), to lay aside our *old self* and put on our *new self* (Ephesians 4:22–24), and to live in a way consistent with our new identity. We are temples of the Holy Spirit who lives within us (1 Corinthians 6:19). Therefore, we have a responsibility to care for and protect that which is God's dwelling place. In order to do this, we must learn to live through Him and allow Him to live freely in and through us.

The core of our identity is a heart that loves God *and* the person He created us to be.

As we apply the *U* step in COURAGE and uncover our true self, we will learn how to embrace our true identity and see ourselves as God sees us.

DISCOVERING OUR GOD-GIVEN WORTH

As founder of Hope for the Heart, a worldwide biblical counseling ministry, June Hunt hosts a live, two-hour call-in counseling program called *Hope in the Night*. She writes and speaks often about our need to see ourselves through God's eyes, as written in 1 Samuel 16:7: "God sees not as man sees, for man looks at the outward appearance, but the LORD looks at the heart." June says:

> To have self-worth is to believe your life has value and significance. . . . God dearly loves each person He creates and has a unique plan and purpose for each life. True self-worth always starts and ends with Him, and never on the perceptions of others. God forever established your worth (over 2,000 years ago) by one act: He gave His Son for you." [7]

Uncover Your True Self

CREATED WITH GOD-GIVEN NEEDS AND FEELINGS

In addition to creating our identity, God has created us with basic, legitimate feelings and needs. If we try to deny those feelings and needs and ignore (or stuff away) the pain that results from not having those basic needs met, we are in danger of building up disappointments that lead to bitterness, that destroy relationships, and affect our self-worth and identity.

WHY WE COVER UP

I bought just about every common lie created by the Four Pests of Pressure—lies we're going to discuss in the *R* step in COURAGE: Replace worldly lies with scriptural truth. I believed if I just tried harder to be good, prayed more, served more, and put more Jesus on top of all my fear, shame, hurt, and sin, everything would simply get better. Unfortunately, it was like putting whipped cream on top of a cake made from a Styrofoam block. No matter how soft and pretty it looked on the outside, the material in the center wasn't authentic.

Are there parts of your life, your identity, you are covering up? Parts you fear will be judged, misunderstood, or simply not accepted? If so, it's time to take a look at why you're hiding.

As I began to uncover the real me, I discovered three basic reasons I was hiding and covering up:

1. My need to *Protect* myself and those I love

2. My need to be *Accepted*

3. My pattern of modeling *Learned behaviors*

These are the three common reasons we mask our reality; I call them our PALs. Unfortunately, these PALs aren't ones we should be hanging around with, because they negatively enable us to hide behind false identities.

95

7 STEPS TO COURAGE

P — Protection

A — Acceptance

L — Learned Behavior

PROTECTION

Physical safety is one of our greatest fundamental needs. When we feel threatened, we often throw logic out the window and jump into survival mode.

I grew up in a household where my dad's mood swings were unpredictable. So it didn't take me long to learn to say and do the right things in order to avoid getting some "sense slapped into me." Verbal abuse and anger were simply a way of life, and as long as my brothers and I were quiet, compliant, and careful, things generally worked out better for us. I also learned early on it was easier on my mom if I kept quiet—if I kept my fears, problems, and worries to myself. The last thing I wanted to do was cause her more pain, so I remained quiet and covered up how I was really feeling when I was hurting or afraid.

ACCEPTANCE

It's important to feel accepted by others. However, it's even more important to accept ourselves, to be okay with who we are, and lay aside the heavy burden of trying to be the person we think others want us to be.

When we attempt to cover up who we are with unhealthy masks in our need for acceptance, we can fall into destructive habits that not only hurt us but also those around us.

In the same way that acceptance drove me to cover up, it had the same negative effect on my father.

Dad was the youngest of nine children growing up in inner city Charlotte under the rule of an alcoholic, abusive father. My father believed in and practiced the religion of hard work from a young age. He was determined to prove he could make something of himself. At age seventeen, my dad lied on an application to the coast guard, was quickly recruited, and relocated to Pennsylvania, where he met and married his first wife. After fulfilling his duties in the coast guard and divorcing his first wife, he returned to Charlotte and took a job selling pots and pans, a perfect job for his charismatic personality. It provided better money than any other job a young man with a ninth-grade education could get.

The driving force behind Dad's success was his desperate need to prove himself so he would be accepted. His driven personality eventually landed him corporate success, and with his success came ego.

In the wrong hands and for the wrong reasons, success and ego can be a dysfunctional duo—a perfect place to hide brokenness, insecurities, and lack of acceptance.

Learned Behavior

Although I know my mother didn't intend to teach me this pattern of behavior, I learned early on the way to survive was simply to pretend nothing was wrong. Albert Bandura, retired professor of social science in psychology at Stanford University, puts it this way:

Most human behavior is learned observationally through modeling: from observing others, one forms an idea of how new behaviors are performed, and on later occasions this coded information serves as a guide for action.[8]

Throughout life we find ourselves in circumstances and relationships that can significantly shape who we are. Our exposure to unhealthy relationships or surroundings can lead us to cover up our true identity and thrust us into a number of unhealthy behaviors as a result.

Exposing Our True Self

A great deal of our success in embracing our identity is dependent upon our willingness to process and overcome painful memories and deep-rooted insecurities.

Author Peter Scazzero says, "It wasn't until the pain exposed how much was hiding under my surface of being a 'good Christian' that it hit me: whole layers of my emotional life had lain buried, untouched by God's transforming power." [9]

Traditionally, X marks the spot where we find treasure. It's at the end of a long journey—the pot of gold at the end of the rainbow. To me, X identifies the areas we must target as we aim to expose who we really are, as we learn how to uncover our true self:

- Exterminate the pests of pressure.

- Examine needs.

- Explore feelings.

- Exchange false masks for true identity.

Exterminate the Pests of Pressure

To live an authentic life, we must exterminate the pests that are feeding on our Four Fundamental Foundations of Health. We first talked about these pests in chapter 4 on overcoming obstacles. Remember, these Four Pests of Pressure are like invisible termites within the walls of our home, eating away at the framework of our life. It bears repeating; although we often don't see them, if left untreated, they will destroy who we are, what we stand for, and why we are here in the first place.

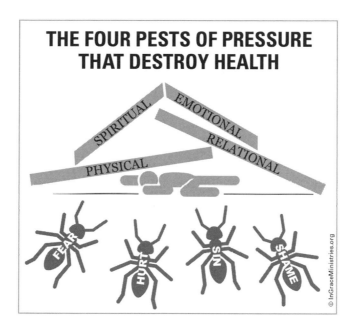

In Ephesians 5:11, God's Word calls us to expose our deeds, beliefs, and behaviors to the light of Christ where His love can shine on them so the truth can be revealed.

My true healing didn't begin until I committed to change and exposed my marriage crisis to Johnny and Janet in Israel. This action started a series of actions that helped me to expose the fear, hurt, shame, and sin that were destroying my life. I had to expose the Four Pests of Pressure to the light of day in order to address and exterminate them.

Examine Needs

The Bible does not hide the flaws and weaknesses of its heroes. Just like us, they had feelings and needs that drove them, sometimes toward success and at other times toward disaster. In either outcome there are valuable lessons to be learned from looking into their lives.

For example, in Romans 7 the apostle Paul took a good look inside himself to observe the reality of the struggles he faced as he strove to live a wholesome life.[10] As he reflected on his feelings of inadequacy, Paul further realized his need of deliverance through Christ. Like Paul, we, too, can learn a great deal about ourselves by looking inside to observe the reality of our feelings and needs.

Being able to uncover our true self is greatly dependent on our ability to understand our basic primary emotional needs. God's Word references these needs often, and I've included some of my favorite verses below:

Love

"Above all these put on love, which binds everything together
in perfect harmony."
— Colossians 3:14 ESV

Safety

"In peace I will lie down and sleep, for you alone, LORD,
make me dwell in safety."
— Psalm 4:8 NIV

Hope

"Now may the God of hope fill you with all joy and peace in believing, so
that you will abound in hope by the power of the Holy Spirit."
— Romans 15:13

Kindness

"Be kind to one another, tender-hearted, forgiving each other,
just as God in Christ also has forgiven you."
— Ephesians 4:32

Uncover Your True Self

Purpose

"I cry out to God Most High, to God who fulfills his purpose for me."
— Psalm 57:2 ESV

EXPLORE FEELINGS

Understanding our needs and carefully inspecting our feelings will help us uncover our true identity.

Have you ever been asked, "What are you *really* feeling?"

This is often a much more difficult question to answer than it seems. It makes a big difference in our ability to understand one another and work through issues when we are able to clearly express what we are really feeling.

God gave us our feelings as warning signals to help us know something in our lives needs to be examined. It is our responsibility to identify what is truly right and what is truly wrong in our lives by several resources: God's Word, godly friends, and a godly counselor.

Reaching a place where we can uncover and identify the levels of our feelings takes time, but it's a process of discovery vital to understanding who we are.

When I began counseling, I didn't understand the importance of digging deeper into underlying emotions that were feeding the ups and downs in my life. I had to learn to identify the difference between secondary feelings and primary feelings. I remember struggling to get below the surface of my anger, depression, and anxiety in order to unearth the primary feelings driving my emotions.

For example, anger is a surface (secondary) feeling.

Who knew?

I had to take time to uncover feelings that were actually causing me to be angry, depressed, and anxious in order to expose my underlying feelings of disappointment, rejection, and fear. When I understood the process better, I learned to express my primary feelings more appropriately and deal with them more effectively.

Secondary, surface feelings, like resentment, bitterness, and worry, are typically easier to identify. In fact, it's in this category of feelings we often get stuck. And when these surface feelings are negative, they generally cause us to say and do things we regret.

Once we are able to identify feelings that are below the surface of our outward emotions, we will be in a better position to manage our responses to our true feelings. This ability, combined with honest communication and healthy boundaries, will allow us to begin experiencing true freedom.

It isn't always easy identifying and effectively communicating our true feelings. Our communication skills can sometimes be lacking, and, quite frankly, the concept of setting healthy boundaries can be a completely foreign concept to some.

Take a look at the two lists on the following page and see if you can identify secondary surface feelings you are struggling with and attempt to match them up with the underlying feelings that are likely provoking them.

As a result of learning to identify my primary feelings, I was able to explain to Mike that my sadness was a result of feelings of loneliness, rejection, and disappointment. Once he understood what I was really feeling deep down, it was easier for him to approach me with care and understanding.

In turn, Mike identified that his anger was fueled by feelings of rejection and disrespect. Although I didn't realize I was being disrespectful, when Mike was able to articulate his feelings, I began to understand how he felt.

As a result of being able to express our underlying feelings, we began to have more compassion for each other, and our communication became more saturated with love.

SURFACE FEELINGS *VS* UNDERYLING FEELINGS

SURFACE FEELINGS	UNDERYLING FEELINGS
Angry	Alienated
Annoyed	Alone
Bitter	Disappointed
Depressed	Dissatisfied
Distrusting	Embarrassed
Embarrassed	Fear (many types)
Frustrated	Frustrated
Furious	Guilty
Insecure	Helpless
Irritated	Hopeless
Jealous	Hurt
Nervous	Lonely
Overwhelmed	Neglected
Paranoid	Rejected
Resentful	Sad
Unforgiving	Shameful
Unhappy	Shocked
Worried	Trapped

© InGraceMinistries.org

7 STEPS TO COURAGE

Exploring our feelings ties in with the ABCs of Change we discussed in chapter 3. Being able to understand our true feelings empowers us to manage them effectively so we don't get caught up in negative attitudes, behaviors, beliefs, circumstances, coping skills, and desires.

Exchange False Masks for True Identity

Wearing a mask involves taking on a role to cover up aspects of our lives we deem unsightly. When our masks cease to work, we often search for another escape, and this is where many of us end up resorting to substance abuse or other abusive behaviors to escape our pain.

There are countless masks we wear to cover up our true identity and conceal our real issues. The exchange of a false mask for a more truthful interpretation of life requires us to let down our defenses and allow ourselves to be fully known.

Read through the list of common masks to see if you can identify any you may wear. Please refer to the chart on page 105.

The Grace of Identity

Once I began the process of uncovering the real me, I discovered there was a whole lot more to uncover than I initially thought. In other words, we don't know what we don't know. In my case, I had been covering up for so many years, it took professional counseling to help me peel back the layers so I could discover *who* and *whose* I really was.

Whether or not we seek professional help, it's important to be willing to extend an abundance of grace and mercy toward ourselves and others as we begin to dig deeper to uncover our true identity and unpack the emotional baggage we've acquired from making fear-based choices.

THE **MASKS**
WE WEAR

1. The Controller:
Attempts to control circumstances and people.

2. The Abuser:
Seeks to demean, hurt, abuse, and suppress others.

3. The Rescuer:
Attempts to rescue others from their pain and issues.

4. The Achiever:
Tries to prove their worth and value by accomplishing tasks.

5. The Imposter:
Pretends to be someone they're not in order to be accepted by others.

6. The Victim:
Allows tragedy to define their identity.

7. The Entertainer:
Attempts to entertain others to gain attention and create distractions.

8. The Pleaser:
Works to gain the approval of others by giving in to them as a result of their own insecurity.

9. The Perfectionist:
Tries to prove their worth and value by attempting to do things perfectly.

10. The Escaper:
Attempts to escape their pain and issues by running away.

© InGraceMinistries.org

This isn't always an easy process; it's not a walk-in-the-park exercise. A hearty dose of grace will contribute greatly to our ability to keep a healthy perspective during the journey.

God's Word defines grace as unmerited favor. In other words, grace is the approval, regard, or preference shown to someone when they don't deserve it. Grace is a concept we often have a hard time embracing, and we're going to talk more about it in "The *E* step in COURAGE: embrace a life of grace."

As you intentionally implement the 7 Steps to COURAGE, ask God to give you the strength to be the person He created you to be, as well as the grace to do it in a way that honors Him.

COURAGE CALL-TO-ACTION STEPS

1. Purchase note cards to use for scripture memorization. Take out four cards, and write the following verses on each: Psalm 139:14 and Ephesians 2:10 and place these cards in common areas where you will see them frequently throughout your day, and read them repeatedly until you have memorized each scripture.

2. Identify any masks you may be wearing and how this may keep you from walking in healthy identity.

3. Take out your notebook or journal and go to a quiet place where you can be alone with God. Go to God in prayer, confessing the areas of your life you are covering up. Ask Him for wisdom and discernment regarding ways you might uncover them. Take at least five to ten minutes, be still, and listen for God to speak to you. Write down what you sense He is encouraging you to do, and then make that your prayer for at least the next seven days.

4. Pray for the courage to embrace transparency and vulnerability around at least a few safe friends.

6

R Step In Courage:
Replace Worldly Lies with Scriptural Truth

Courage is being able to admit we've been wrong.

"We demolish arguments and every pretension that sets itself up against the knowledge of God, and we take captive every thought to make it obedient to Christ.".

—2 Corinthians 10:5 NIV

*g*rowing up, my family lived in a swim, tennis, and golf community. I was introduced to the deep end of the pool by a swim instructor when I was a toddler. I learned the edges of the pool first, the safety of the steps, and how to kick my feet in rhythm. It didn't take me long to start exploring the depths. There was no panic, just the exhilarating rush of freedom as I flew beneath the surface. The cold water soon became a welcome greeting to my days, and it wasn't long until I was swimming competitively. I felt secure navigating this liquid terrain. It was a place of adventure and joy. The very idea of drowning never occurred to me. I believed that if I kicked, paddled, or floated, I could always keep my head above water.

7 STEPS TO COURAGE

When I found myself in Israel drowning in fear, I had a choice: sink or swim.

Inherently, I knew what to do—I chose to swim.

This was a choice that set a course of change into motion that caused me to question, challenge, and alter a significant number of false beliefs I had grown to accept as truth.

Have you ever found yourself in a place where life takes a turn and suddenly you are in a situation you never dreamed you'd be in? A place where questions outnumber answers and the lines between lies and truth are no longer crisp and clear?

We all have beliefs and points of view we learn as we're growing up. As we experience life, we retain or discard various belief systems. I love what author Brené Brown says about this:

> What we learn about ourselves and how we learn to engage the world as children sets a course that either will require us to spend a significant part of our life fighting to reclaim our self-worth or will give us hope, courage, and resilience for our journeys.[1]

As I took the *R* step in COURAGE and began to replace worldly lies with scriptural truth, I began the process of reclaiming the self-worth I had lost and finding a level of hope, courage, and resilience I had never known.

I invite you to join me in this life-changing adventure.

ACCEPTING OUR DISTORTED REALITY AS TRUTH

I learned a lot of things as a child, some healthy, and some not so much.

Mom was an antiques dealer with an exceptional eye for beauty, and she created an eclectic and gorgeous home. She was strong and expected me to be strong. There was no room for showing weakness or fear in our home. Like many women from her generation, she did not acknowledge, much less ever discuss, her often-volatile marriage or the challenges she faced.

I experienced a lot of fear and confusion as a child, but I learned at the same time it was not acceptable to express either one, so I didn't—not to anyone in or outside my family. I simply learned to survive the hurtful, frightening, and confusing times by going into survival mode and telling myself things would get better. In essence, I mirrored my mother's behavior.

As a result, I unknowingly adopted the worldly lie that *it's best to hide pain, problems, and pressure, and just pretend everything is okay.*

At the time, I believed this "truth" without question. Often, what we perceive as truth becomes a pattern of belief we carry throughout life. A belief is an expression of what we *think* is true. The operative word being, *think*.

The problem is, not everything we perceive, learn, discover, or think is actually true. In some cases, there are even things we see with our own eyes that aren't true (can you say *Hollywood*?).

As we grow, we become more independent and develop a more conscious awareness of our personal ability to make choices, particularly with respect to our beliefs. But as youngsters, our understanding of being able to choose a particular belief is limited. We tend to model our beliefs on the behavior of others.

Like my mother, I assimilated a pattern of pretending that my emotionally painful experiences simply didn't happen. In doing so, I allowed the Four Pests of Pressure to have unlimited access to the tender parts of my heart and soul. Completely unaware, I nurtured an environment where fear, shame, hurt, and sin could multiply without question, without boundaries. That is, until the day I found myself in a hotel room in Israel and decided enough was enough.

7 STEPS TO COURAGE

THE SPIRITUAL AND SCRIPTURAL CONNECTION

In discovering spiritual truth through the Scriptures, the first belief we must accept, trust, and understand is that the Bible is inspired, authoritative, and inerrant.

The inerrancy of Scripture refers to the fact the Bible is always true[2] and free from any "falsehood, fraud, and deceit."[3] What the Bible says about any particular topic is true.

God inspired humans with various backgrounds, personalities, writing styles, and cultural contexts to write His Word down. Scripture is God breathed (2 Timothy 3:16), not written by the impulse of man, but a result of the Holy Spirit speaking to men (2 Peter 1:21).

The Bible is unique in that it was written over a fifteen-hundred-year span by more than forty authors from all walks of life, in multiple languages and on three different continents.[4] Yet despite that, the consistency of biblical content is remarkable. Evidence in the form of archaeology, secular historical records, and thousands of manuscripts exists to support its truthfulness, along with unlimited accounts of how God's Word has transformed the lives of men, women, and children throughout history.

Consequently, when we disbelieve or disobey God's Word, we disbelieve or disobey God. Since God's Word is absolute truth, His Word must be the authority in our lives.

When we read the Bible with an open heart, the Holy Spirit will speak to our own spirit—our own heart—and affirm that the words of Scripture are the very words of God Himself and must, therefore, be the authority for our lives.

Throughout life, we are exposed to false doctrine and misunderstandings of God's Word, whether by well-meaning friends, teachers, or even biblical scholars. These distortions can often put us in vulnerable positions when we attempt to base some of life's most important decisions around these distorted beliefs. When I began counseling, I didn't realize how many worldly lies I had adopted throughout the years, even ones I believed were scriptural.

There is no doubt in my mind, the sheer immensity of my delusional false reality is one of the primary reasons God has drawn me to in-depth Bible study over the years. He was completely aware that He needed to ground me in biblical truth in order to help me recognize the lies and prepare me to be a spokesperson for kingdom work.

From the moment we surrender our life to Christ, we embark on our journey of sanctification, the process by which we are transformed to become more like Christ.[5] Through the work of the Holy Spirit and our growth in the knowledge and understanding of God's Word, we are continually transformed into the women and men of God that He calls us to be. When we neglect the study of God's Word, we settle for spiritual growth that is slow and full of stumbling blocks. But when we study, understand, and apply God's Word to our lives, we begin to exchange a stagnant (or slow-paced) spiritual growth journey for a steady and fulfilling one that will bring glory to God and transformation to our lives.

The Bible says, "My people are destroyed for lack of knowledge."[6]

On our journey to live courageous lives, we must pray for wisdom and discernment. We must continually seek knowledge from God's Word, from the Book of Life. It's vitally important for us to read and study the Bible regularly and work hard to accurately interpret it so we can properly apply it and be in a better position to discern worldly lies from scriptural truth.

7 STEPS TO COURAGE

EXCHANGING DISTORTED BELIEFS

Author Peter Scazerro says, "You can't have true peace in Christ's kingdom with lies and pretense. They must be exposed to the light and replaced with the truth."[7]

It's quite telling how often the need to expose our secrets—our lies—comes up when we're trying to find courage. When God is really convicting us to change, when we've really reached the pivotal place where we stop hiding and start seeking, it quickly becomes evident that God's ultimate goal is to lead us to replace worldly lies with scriptural truth.

We don't have to be in the midst of a crisis to realize the need to identify and overcome lies we have accepted as truth. Unfortunately, that's usually what it takes for us to do so.

Lies feed into our fear, shame, hurt, and sin. That said, as we take the *R* step in COURAGE, we need to exterminate the Four Pests of Pressure and shore up our Four Fundamental Foundations of Health. Finding courage will always come back to an awareness of these two key areas in life.

Always.

WE'RE ONLY HUMAN

We are all susceptible to adopting false beliefs—lies—which can cause us to make unhealthy choices in life. When these lies are repeated over and over in our minds by our inner accuser, we are left vulnerable to unhealthy feelings, irrational thinking, poor attitudes, and inappropriate actions. In other words, the parasitic pests—the insects of insecurity—are feeding on the very foundation of our soul. Refer to the illustrated charts on the following page.

When we begin to look closely at our feelings and needs, identify the masks we wear, and intentionally challenge the things we believe (or thought we

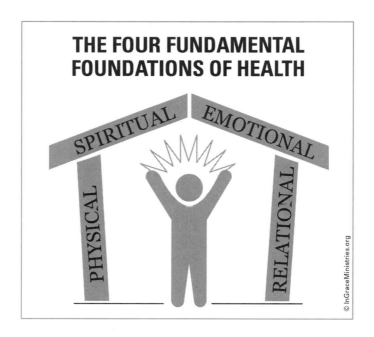

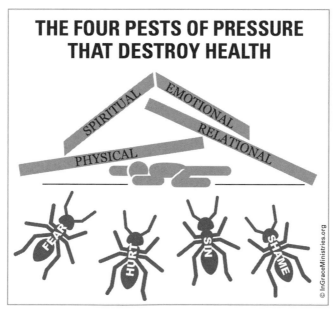

believed), we are often faced with monumental choices. During these seasons of change, we can sometimes receive new information that challenges our old beliefs. When this occurs, it's up to us to choose:

1. Accept it (believe it).

2. Ignore it (deny it).

3. Question it (challenge it).

4. Blend it (merge it into our current belief).

5. Replace it (change what we believe entirely).

Ultimately, the choice is ours whether or not we embrace our ability to choose.

Alas, there will always be those tortured souls who feel they have no choice, who feel they are at the mercy of fate, responsibility, or guilt. There are people who have succumbed to the devastating destruction that comes after years and years of living with the Four Pests of Pressure.

THE TRUTH TRIFECTA

When we develop a keen ability to discern lies in our life and replace them with spiritual truth—scriptural truth—we will greatly reduce the impact the Four Pests of Pressure have on our Four Fundamental Foundations of Health. When we exterminate fear, shame, hurt, and sin from our lives, we become stronger. When we strive to develop our spiritual, emotional, relational, and physical foundations, we can better embrace our true identity and walk in God's will for our life.

Our ability to make fearless, healthy choices is directly related to what we believe. Author Chris Thurman says, "Every lie that goes through your mind is slow, self-inflicted psychological and spiritual death." [8]

Replace Worldly Lies with Scriptural Truth

I ask you, isn't it time to blow these lies out of the water?

How do we know if something we believe is, in fact, a lie?

How can we replace the lies in our life with scriptural truth? How do we change a faulty belief system? Remember, a belief is what we *think* is true about an aspect of our reality and is motivated by some evidence or reason. Therefore, we can't simply choose to believe or not believe something. To successfully change our beliefs involves a process of identifying lies, discovering trustworthy information that influences us to let go of the lies, and adopting new accurate beliefs.[9]

Following is the three-step process of discovery I learned as God walked me through the 7 Steps to COURAGE.

The Truth Trifecta

Step 1: Identify worldly lies.

Step 2: Challenge worldly lies with scriptural truth.

Step 3: Replace false beliefs with new beliefs.

Three simple steps. Sounds easy, doesn't it?

The truth is, any change can be hard. This particular change, however, can be especially problematic because it's an area where Satan desperately wants to keep us in bondage. Yet with God's help and Holy Spirit guidance (and with the right tools and right attitude), making intentional choices to change is possible.

Let's look at how to implement the Truth Trifecta, beginning with the first step.

7 STEPS TO COURAGE

Step 1: Identify worldly lies.

Whew.

This could take a longgggg time.

We believe countless lies; it's impossible to list them all here. But there is a common denominator in identifying a worldly lie.

Here it is: if we are walking in bondage to fear-based choices, if we feel hopeless and worthless, and if emotional pain is an almost constant companion, there's a good chance our belief system is skewed.

Every lie we believe has a direct effect on our Four Fundamental Foundations of Health: our spiritual, emotional, relational, and physical health. Every lie we believe feeds the Four Pests of Pressure and keeps fear, shame, hurt, and sin alive.

Perhaps worldly lies have been told to you (or modeled by influential people) at some point in your life, or maybe you simply adopted them along the way without even realizing it. Regardless of how they come to us, we must recognize faulty belief systems as lies that attack our identity, steal our joy, and keep us in fearful bondage. And we must replace them with scriptural truth from God's Word.

Step 2: Challenge worldly lies with scriptural truth.

Just because we have a Bible or two on our bookshelves doesn't mean God's Word is being transported by osmosis into our brain.

Please forgive me if that sounds harsh.

We have to actually read, study, compare, and apply the wisdom and knowledge it contains. We have to discover for ourselves what is actually written in God's Word and open our hearts and minds to the power of the Holy Spirit to convict us to challenge what we think is true.

Replace Worldly Lies with Scriptural Truth

I often say, "God's Word is transformational but only at the pace and depth by which we expose ourselves to it."

Once we identify the lies we have adopted and discover scriptural truth through Bible study, we are then able to move on to the final step in the Truth Trifecta.

Step 3: Replace false beliefs with new beliefs.

The worldly lies we believe hinder our ability to change our negative behaviors, attack our self-worth, and often leave us feeling hopeless. They contribute to the fear-based choices we make. They keep us from saying "yes" to positive changes and "no" to negative influences. They keep us from being spiritually healthy.

Worldly lies must be eliminated from our belief system.

My counselor recommended an exercise that helped me tremendously with this process. He encouraged me to write down my lies and truths on paper and read through them daily for sixty days.

That's right—daily for two months.

That way, the truth I discovered would become embedded in my mind. And when I was tempted to believe one of my worldly lies, I could quickly recall God's scriptural truth and base my feelings, thoughts, attitudes, actions, and reactions on the new truth I had committed to memory.

This was (and is) an incredible and valuable exercise.

I struggled with many of these deceptions for decades until God got my attention and sobered me up from the intoxication of so many lies.

With the help of my counselor, I realized the distortion of my beliefs, and I began to discover and accept the scriptural truth that cancelled out the worldly lies. With the help of my heavenly Father, I have been able to live a far more courageous life, and I've discovered grace in a new and fresh way.

7 STEPS TO COURAGE

Every step to courage I've walked has been life changing. But the *R* step in COURAGE: Replace worldly lies with scriptural truth, set me on a course that entirely changed my perspective about God, as God's Word changed me from within.

Let's look at the list of Top 20 Worldly Lies We Believe. Do any of them resonate in your spirit? When you finish reading this list, grab your notebook or journal and begin to identify your own worldly lies.

Then, on the following pages, look at what God's Word says about these lies in my list of scriptural Top 20 Truths That Replace Worldly Lies.

Top 20 Worldly Lies We Believe

1. I'm not good enough.
2. I need the approval of others to be valuable.
3. I am responsible for the actions and behaviors of others.
4. I can't say no with firmness and love and yes with honest authenticity.
5. God and me, that's all I need.
6. I need to hide pain, problems, and pressure.
7. I need to care for others and neglect my own God-given needs.
8. My relationships should meet all my needs.
9. The more I serve, the more God will love me.
10. My unhappiness is someone else's fault.
11. I only need to attend church to be spiritually healthy.
12. I have to accept being abused.
13. Life should be fair.
14. Other people should think and act like I do.
15. It's okay to care-take and enable others in their negative behaviors.
16. I can handle the stress; it's not really hurting me.
17. God should protect me from pain and suffering.
18. My problems are all my fault.
19. My physical health is not important.
20. If I sin, I must not be saved.

© InGraceMinistries.org

Top 20 Truths That Replace Worldly Lies

1. I am valuable and adequate for every good work.
    (Psalm 139:14; Ephesians 2:10)

2. God values me and loves me unconditionally.
    (Romans 5:8; Galatians 1:10)

3. Each person is responsible for his or her own actions
    and behaviors. (Ezekiel 18:20)

4. I can say no with firmness and love and yes with honest
    authenticity. (Matthew 5:37; Ephesians 4:15)

5. I need God and I need other safe people to care for me,
    cry with me, encourage me, warn me, pray for me, and
    accept me. (Romans 12:15-16; 1 Corinthians 12:25)

6. I need to confess my pain, problems, and pressure to
    safe people who will counsel, encourage, care, and pray
    for me. (1 Thessalonians 5:11; James 5:16)

7. I need to care for others and care for my God-given
    needs. (Matthew 22:39)

8. My relationships will never meet all my needs—God
    meets all my needs according to His riches in glory in
    Christ Jesus. (2 Corinthians 12:9; Philippians 4:19)

9. God loves me unconditionally—not because of what
    I do. (John 3:16; Ephesians 2:8-9)

10. My happiness is my responsibility—it can be found in
    my relationship with God. (Psalm 16:11; 1 Peter 4:12-14)

(continued...)

(Top 20 Truths That Replace Worldly Lies - con't.)

11. I need to spend quiet time with God in prayer, read and study His Word, and fellowship with other Christians to be spiritually healthy. (Jude 1:20; Psalm 1:1–2; 2 Timothy 2:15; 3:16–17)

12. I deserve to be treated with kindness and care, and I need to set healthy boundaries when necessary. (Romans 12:18; Ephesians 5:25; 1 Thessalonians 5:21–22)

13. We live in a sinful world and therefore I need to expect difficulties in life. (Matthew 5:45; James 1:2–4)

14. We are all at different places of growth and development, therefore we often differ in our thoughts and actions. (Matthew 7:1–5; Romans 12:4–13; 14:1)

15. It's beneficial to both me and the person with unhealthy behaviors to set boundaries, maintain them, and allow them to experience consequences in order to help them grow. (Matthew 18:15–17; Galatians 6:7; Ephesians 6:4)

16. I need to put away worry and trust God with my circumstances. (Matthew 6:27; Philippians 4:6–7; 1 Peter 5:7)

17. I can endure suffering with a positive attitude. (Romans 5:3; Hebrews 10:36; James 1:2)

18. My problems may come from my choices, the choices of others, or trials. (John 16:33; Ephesians 6:12; 2 Timothy 3:1–17)

19. Good health goes well with my soul; therefore I need to take care of my body for it is the dwelling place of the Holy Spirit. (1 Corinthians 6:19–20; 3 John 1:2)

20. I must stay close to God and rely on Him to help me resist sin, and I must repent and return to a right relationship with God when I do sin. (Acts 3:19; 1 Corinthians 10:13; 1 John 1:9)

© InGraceMinistries.org

COURAGE CALL-TO-ACTION STEPS

1. Before opening your Bible, pray for God to convict you of any worldly lies you believe. Then look up the following passages in your Bible and read them daily until you have committed them to memory.

   a. Colossians 2:8

   b. 2 Corinthians 10:5

   c. Proverbs 3:5–6

2. Take out your notebook or journal and draw a line down the middle of a page to make two columns. In the first column make a list of lies you believe and in the second column write out the scriptures you've discovered that replace the lies. Caution: Don't attempt to make Scripture fit your belief. Instead, conform your belief to fit the truth found in Scripture.

3. Read those lies and truths at least once a day and meditate on denouncing the lies in the name of Jesus and accepting the truths. Do this exercise for at least thirty days, but preferably for sixty days.

4. Seek out a spiritually mature Christian and ask to meet with her weekly for discipleship over the course of this exercise in order to strengthen your understanding of biblical truth. If possible, maintain this relationship after the allotted time.

7

A Step in Courage:
Accept the Things You Cannot Change

Courage is accepting things we cannot change and changing the things we can.

*"For everything there is a season, and a time for every matter under heaven;
a time to seek, and a time to lose; a time to keep, and a time to cast away."*
—*Ecclesiastes 3:1, 6 ESV*

Our past can really complicate our present, if we let it.

Sadly, we can't change our past, but we can work to identify how and why we have allowed past issues to affect our lives today. What we *can* do is stop the vicious cycle that keeps us from walking in freedom and living the life God has for us.

Sometimes we don't fully understand how events from our past have contributed to a faulty belief system or have established triggers that cause us to operate in fear, shame, hurt, or sin in our present. Sometimes our memories are too painful to consciously remember, so we subconsciously block them out. Yet they exist and can negatively affect our attitudes, behaviors, beliefs, circumstances, coping skills, desires, and emotions.

7 STEPS TO COURAGE

Being able to emotionally explore the challenging events of our past and put them behind us takes hard work and commitment. However, knowing the root issues and doing something about changing them are two entirely different things.

Being able to accept the things you cannot change does not mean you will forever be shackled to accepting your lot in life. Accepting does not mean settling.

The Serenity Prayer is the common name for an originally untitled prayer by the theologian Reinhold Niebuhr. It's a prayer about learning how to accept and has been adopted by Alcoholics Anonymous and other twelve-step programs. Chances are you've heard all or part of this well-known prayer over the course of your life. It's a long prayer, but this is the part quoted most often:

> "God, grant me the serenity to accept the things I cannot change, the courage to change the things I can, and the wisdom to know the difference."[1]

There was a time I thought it was impossible to have serenity, courage, and wisdom. I was too lost, too broken, and frankly, too tired to even try.

Thankfully, God wasn't.

CHANGEABLE AND UNCHANGEABLE

In order to identify and overcome issues that negatively impact our lives, we need to discern the difference between who and what we can and cannot change. Understanding these differences is critical in our journey to realize what to accept and what to proactively change.

Let's look at the lists of common Changeable versus Unchangeable life experiences.

CHANGEABLE VS UNCHANGEABLE

CHANGEABLE	UNCHANGEABLE
• How we see and love God	• How God sees and loves us
• Our reponse to the past	• Our past
• Our response to the actions/choices of others	• The actions/choices of others
• Sin by us	• Sin by others
• What we know and believe	• What others know or believe
• Our response to each season	• The natural seasons of life
• How we take care of ourselves	• Our genetics

© InGraceMinistries.org

7 STEPS TO COURAGE

ACCEPTING HOW GOD SEES AND LOVES US

We've talked about our identity in Christ and how God sees us throughout the pages of this book. It's a primary component in our ability to make fearless choices and walk in grace. God created us, loves us, saved us, and is always working in, through, and on us.

Few of us have had perfect lives, and comparatively speaking mine was privileged and blessed. I think of the women I met on my trip to India. They accept the fact they have been born into a country and culture that devalues women, but they do not settle for that view. Many of them have lived in unimaginable conditions, yet they are able to accept how God sees and loves them with a courageousness that makes me weep.

ACCEPTING OUR PAST

About a year after I was born, my mom began to see a different side of my dad—a man whose greatest priorities were being financially successful and getting his wants, needs, and desires met. His insecurities drove him to purchase homes, cars, and other possessions to portray a certain image. He put pressure on Mom to look and act a certain way and used anger and intimidation to get his family to do what he wanted.

I have good memories of laughter, warmth, and security during my early years. But they are also mixed with bad memories of fear, hurt, and confusion. I think this combination of good and bad is true for many of us.

I dearly loved my parents, but they were broken, just as I have been. While I can't change what happened in my past or my memories, I can change how I choose to respond to those issues today. Through God's amazing grace (and intentional effort on my part), I've been able to stop the negative effect these issues have on my life and relationships.

Accept the Things You Cannot Change

If our past includes particularly painful aspects or memories that continue to bubble up and affect our present, we must identify and deal with any leftover pain in order to move toward freedom and live a courageous life.

While we cannot change our past, we *can* change how we respond to it.

With the help of a professional counselor, I was able to change my responses and deal with the residual pain by addressing nine areas in life. We can break free from the bondage of past trauma and sin when we make the choice to implement these steps, develop our personal relationship with Christ, and connect with counselors and others who can support us.

I feel confident these Nine Steps to Dealing with Pain can help you, too.

On the following page, let's take a look at the chart LifeBuilders counselor Robbie Goss has provided.

ACCEPTING THE ACTIONS AND CHOICES OF OTHERS

My father was a successful salesman and manager in a large corporation. We never had to struggle much for material things, but financial freedom does not guarantee love, security, and happiness.

The unfortunate reality is, my father courted my mother with many promises of those key ingredients: love, security, and a life of happiness. Alas, because of unprocessed brokenness in his own life, he was unable to live up to some of those promises. My dad lived with emotional damage from an abusive childhood that trapped him in consistently negative behavior patterns.

Mom never shared her pain, but I do remember one time when I was a little girl she threatened to divorce my dad. It was the only time I ever saw him cry. The issue was over how he was treating my brothers. By the end of their discussion, my dad promised to do better, a promise that was short-lived. While the issues changed over the years, the empty promises did not.

Nine Steps to Dealing with Pain

1. Allow myself to feel the full weight of the pain (Psalm 126:5).

2. Express my primary emotions to God and trusted, safe friends (Philippians 4:6; James 5:13–16).

3. Recognize the original source of my pain (abandonment, abuse, or traumatic events) (Proverbs 4:34).

4. Receive healing from the Lord for my specific damaged feelings (Luke 4:18).

5. Release my pain back to the cross (Isaiah 53:4–5).

6. Rescue the part of me I rejected at the point of my pain (Proverbs 19:7).

7. Reject the lies that came from my pain (Romans 12:2).

8. Replace my lies with specific truth (Romans 12:2).

9. Release my offenders by forgiving them (Hebrews 12:15).

© InGraceMinistries.org

Accept the Things You Cannot Change

Sadly, my mother was trapped in her own dysfunctional denial. She ignored her better judgment and personal truth and consistently settled for my father's negative choices. It took her twenty-five years to change the one thing she could: herself.

In the *C* step in COURAGE: Commit to change, we talked about the need to focus on changing the one person you can change: you. While we can encourage and influence others, we must realize the decision of how they believe, behave, act, or react is completely up to them.

Mom needed to let go of trying to change my father and do the only thing she could have done under the circumstances: seek help for herself and her children. She desperately needed the "courage to change the things she could," such as responding to her husband and allowing both of their issues to negatively impact us.

I repeated this similar pattern with Mike. When a crisis arose in our marriage, I would either voice empty threats or simply resign myself to believe things weren't going to change, so I might as well accept it (or settle) and go on.

But being able to take the *A* step in COURAGE: Accept the things you cannot change, doesn't mean you settle for the way things are. It means you get smart and stop trying to change anyone else's behavior or choices. It means you change your focus and shine the light of new direction on yourself.

I can't change what happened, and I can't change the fact that my parents both made choices that sometimes hurt me, but I can change how I let my memories affect me. I can work to forgive Mom and Dad for their negative choices and choose to focus on my loving memories.

Forgiveness plays a significant part in making fearless choices and walking in grace. Learning to forgive ourselves and others, without compromising healthy boundaries, is something we *can* change.

7 STEPS TO COURAGE

ACCEPTING THE REALITY OF SIN

Sin. It's a little word that can pack a powerful punch.

We can't change the fact that others are going to sin against us or that sin in the world impacts our lives daily. Sin always has consequences, and consequences of sin always impact more people than just the sinner. We live in a fallen world. Therefore, throughout our lives we will go through various trials, struggles, and periods of suffering simply because someone else made a sinful choice along the way.

The one sin experience we *can* change is how we handle our personal temptation to sin.

The Bible says we are all sinners in need of a Savior.[2] Christians and non-Christians alike are tempted and fall into sin every single day. But there are safeguards we can put into place that will strengthen our ability to resist our temptation to sin.

We must first and foremost ensure that our salvation is in place. One of the greatest tragedies can be a false sense of security in a salvation that never actually took place. "Pay close attention to yourself and to your teaching; persevere in these things, for as you do this you will ensure salvation both for yourself and for those who hear you."[3]

Once our salvation is sealed, it's important to develop habits that will help us grow in our knowledge and understanding of God and His Word. It's always concerned me how gung ho some Christians are to lead others to the cross but then expect them to know everything about being a Christian by some kind of miraculous osmosis.

Alas, it doesn't happen that way.

If we implement daily prayer time with the Lord, study His Word, and surround ourselves with godly influences and accountability, we can strengthen our awareness of God's power and thus strengthen our defenses against sin. The closer we grow to God, the easier it will be to resist the temptation to sin. But because we're human, it's highly unlikely any earthly routine is going to completely keep us from ever falling into temptation and sin.

We must accept the fact that sin will always be a stumbling block in life. But by exercising healthy habits, we can change our outlook on it, put safeguards in place so we can increase our ability to resist it, and more properly manage its impact.

Accepting Our Uniqueness

The fact that we are completely unique individuals designed and created with individual style, looks, personalities, and features, is something we cannot change, even if we try. Short of reconstructive surgery, there is no changing the physical characteristics that have been passed down to us from one generation to another. Likewise, some diseases and health conditions can also run in families.

By accepting our God-given uniqueness and recognizing our natural-born gifts and talents, we can accept the things about ourselves we cannot change and employ our personal strengths.

By understanding our inherited traits and family health history, our doctors can help us develop targeted health plans. We can't change our genetic predisposition, but we can change our diet, exercise, and awareness of our nutritional needs.

Accepting What Others Know or Believe

Often there's a disparity between what others know or believe and what we know and believe. For the most part, we all experience life differently, we learn differently, and we all grow in our knowledge, understanding, and beliefs at an individual pace. Whether it's religion, politics, or brand loyalty, we all have varying opinions and beliefs—things that may never change. What can change is how we approach people who think and believe differently than us.

God's Word calls us to be patient, understanding, and nonjudgmental of others, to measure everything against the plumb line of His Word, and to speak truth *in love*. This is particularly important when approaching others who have thoughts and beliefs that don't line up with ours. Walking in grace is never exhibited more than when we are faced with someone who doesn't agree with us.

The Bible says, "Do not judge, and you will not be judged; and do not condemn, and you will not be condemned; pardon, and you will be pardoned."[4] It is important we not judge someone whom we *think* isn't at the same spiritual, emotional, relational, or intellectual place we are. The fact is, we may be unfairly judging that person. Plus, God commands us not to judge, because our judgment may discourage others from any possible growth, and we will most likely diminish our relationship with them in the long run. "We urge you, brethren, admonish the unruly, encourage the fainthearted, help the weak, *be patient with everyone.*"[5]

We must strive to accept others where they are, speak the truth in love to them, and, above all, we must exercise nonjudgment, patience, and grace.

ACCEPTING THE SEASONS OF LIFE

The Bible says, "God controls the times and seasons."[6]

The first season of our life is infancy through early childhood. Then we move from early childhood through adolescence. During these two seasons, we are very impressionable. We are growing, learning, and developing our understanding of what life is all about. At the same time, our belief system is being developed, beliefs about who we are and why we exist. We are learning what is acceptable and unacceptable in our cultural surroundings. What we learn and believe during these critical developmental seasons can have a profound effect on the choices we make throughout the rest of our lives.

During the next season of early adulthood most of us leave home for the first time, start careers, get married, and have children. This is typically a busy season of life where our primary focus is on jobs, relationships, and children.

The next season of life is often referred to as midlife. Those with children become empty nesters; friends and family members begin to pass away. And we begin to realize how short life is and slow down a little, often taking inventory of our lives. This is a stage where many of us begin to think seriously about where we are in life—and where we want to go. This is typically when we begin to think about our legacy, how our lives will impact the next generation, and how much time we have left to set goals and take actions that will enable us to realize our wishes and dreams.

The final season in life is sometimes referred to as late adulthood. As we enter this season, we are faced with the limitations and challenges that come as our bodies and health begin to change.

The Bible says there is a season for everything. What season do you find yourself in now? Newly married? Raising young children? Single? Divorced? Widowed? Empty nester? Growing older?

No matter the season, God is in the midst of it, and His greatest desire is for us to surrender each and every season of life to Him.

We live in a culture where unbelievable opportunities exist to push the boundaries of limitations brought on by the passing seasons of time. As we progress through the seasons of life, it's good to pray for wisdom and discernment concerning our choices.

The apostle Paul said, "Therefore be careful how you walk, not as unwise men but as wise, making the most of your time."[7]

Time is a gift from God, a gift we should not waste.

7 STEPS TO COURAGE

It takes courage to accept our present season of life and celebrate the blessings—and even the challenges—it brings.

Joy comes from being at peace with God, ourselves, and others in all seasons of life.

COURAGE TO CHANGE THE THINGS YOU CAN
AND THE WISDOM TO KNOW THE DIFFERENCE

Yes, there are some things we can never change. Fortunately, the choices we make now don't fall into this category.

We can choose to live a life where the poor choices we or others have made no longer control us. When we fully grasp the *A* step in COURAGE: Accept the things you cannot change, we take a giant step forward in our ability to make fearless choices.

Accepting the changeable versus the unchangeable is an ever-present challenge in our lives. Yet it's one we can overcome as we implement each of the 7 Steps to COURAGE and grow closer to God in the process.

ACCEPTING SALVATION

When it comes to things we cannot change, there is one element that will forever hold the top position: We cannot change how much God loves us, how He longs to protect, provide, and guide us. We cannot change how passionate He is to save us.

If you are unsure about your salvation, or if you've never prayed to receive Christ, there's no better time than now to make that life-changing decision and invite Jesus Christ to be your personal Lord and Savior.

We were members of a local neighborhood church when I was a child, and we attended fairly regularly. Although I have memories of attending church with my mother, I can't tell you I received biblical instruction that served as a

Accept the Things You Cannot Change

firm foundation in my future relationship with the Lord. Honestly, I feel the foundation I had was somewhat distorted and may have actually hindered my progress as a believer after my true conversion years later.

I grew up believing I was a Christian and was therefore heaven-bound. It wasn't until I was in my late teens that someone challenged me regarding my salvation, and I made the decision to truly surrender my life to Christ.

If you have never asked Christ into your life, or if you have any doubt as to whether you have completely surrendered your life to our Creator, I invite you to do so today by praying the short prayer below. This isn't a step to be taken lightly, and what may seem to be a simple prayer can completely change the course of your life forever when it comes from a genuine place in your heart.

Dear Lord,

I humbly confess to You that I am a sinner. I have lived my life by following my own selfish wants and desires. I come before You today and ask You to forgive me of my sins, believing that You died on the cross to pay for them in full. You did for me what I am not able to do for myself. Therefore, today I am receiving You, Jesus, as Lord and Savior of my life, to take up residence in my soul and to cover me with Your abundant grace and mercy. I choose today to follow You and to turn my life over to You. Lord, I'm really not sure what this looks like in its entirety, but I'm going to trust You to open the eyes and ears of my heart and walk with me every step of the way.

I love you, Jesus, and I thank you that I am Your child. Amen.

If you sincerely recited this prayer just now, whether aloud or in the silence of your heart, I truly want to be the first person to welcome you into the family of God. Accepting the salvation offered by Jesus Christ is the most courageous step you will ever take.

COURAGE CALL-TO-ACTION STEPS

1. Take out two notecards and write the Serenity Prayer on each one. Place these cards in the same areas you placed your Scripture memorization note cards. Pray this prayer daily for at least seven days and strive to memorize it.

2. Spend time in prayer and communication with God. Ask Him to give you the wisdom to discern the things you can and cannot change.

3. Take out your notebook or journal and make two columns. Write "Cannot Change" at the top of the first column and "Can Change" at the top of the second column. List the specific things you can and cannot change in your life.

8

9 Step in Courage: Grasp God's Love for You

Courage is accepting God's view over all others.

"I'm absolutely convinced that nothing—nothing living or dead, angelic or demonic, today or tomorrow, high or low, thinkable or unthinkable—absolutely nothing can get between us and God's love because of the way that Jesus our Master has embraced us."

—Romans 8:38–39 MSG

*I*t's difficult *not* to have courage when we fully grasp how deep God's love is for us.

And as the Bible says, "If God is for us, who is against us?"[1]

When I was saved at age nineteen, my eternity was sealed. But my spiritual growth was just beginning. I knew little about the depth of God's love for me, and I had no clue as to why I needed to understand it. Over the years following, my walk with the Lord moved at a snail's pace, until difficulties in life caused me to develop a desperate need for a closer relationship with Christ.

I've experienced quite a few life storms over the years, storms that drove me into the arms of God desperately seeking shelter. Looking back, I can see how God used those storms to help me grasp the magnitude of His love. Without

His presence providing love, comfort, and reassurance during those times, I am convinced I would have fallen into even greater sin and suffering.

Eventually, I began to study His Word with more prayerful intention, and the deeper I dug, the more I fell in love. And the more I fell in love, the deeper I wanted to go. The more I studied, the more I grasped God's love and relationship with humankind.

Without a personal relationship with the Creator of this universe, we are walking through life veiled to the possibilities of all God has in store for us. With a personal relationship, we are promised an abundance of joy, hope, peace, and love—everything we need to find our courage: "Now may the God of hope fill you with all joy and peace in believing, so that you will abound in hope by the power of the Holy Spirit."[2]

How We See God

Our spiritual growth is a journey we begin when we receive Christ as our personal Lord and Savior. While God will equip us with all we need, it's up to us to determine the pace of that journey. From my personal experience, I know in order to fully grasp God's love for us, we must grow in our understanding of God and strengthen our relationship with Him.

Our spiritual journey begins long before we are born. Our physical journey on earth begins when we take our first breath outside of our mother's womb. Our life's journey, however, cannot be summed up as easily, as it changes throughout the four stages of how we see God:

1. Seeing

2. Believing

3. Accepting

4. Surrendering

Grasp God's Love for You

1. *Seeing God.* As children, we generally see God in a simplistic view. Depending on influences from our environment, we might see God as a superhero, father figure, loving friend, harsh judge, or someone simply out there somewhere. As we grow, we are exposed to more information about God's existence. We may or may not be introduced to the basic concepts of our Creator, of heaven and hell, and of the life, death, burial, and resurrection of Christ.

But whether we see Him or not, God exists.

2. *Believing in God.* When we are children, believing comes more naturally, as our hearts and minds are often more open than when we become adults. Believing in God brings us hope, peace, joy, and the reassurance we are never alone. Depending on what we see and choose to believe about God, it is at this stage we generally accept or deny Jesus as our personal Lord and Savior. Sometimes we choose to believe, and we stop there, having checked the box of salvation, our ticket to heaven, thinking we've gone far enough. When we do this, we miss out on the immense blessings that are a direct result of our spiritual growth and close relationship with God.

3. *Accepting God.* When a door opened for Mike to begin working in the insurance industry at a young age, his natural charisma and high work ethic propelled him forward at an amazing speed. I joined him at age nineteen and began selling insurance, door to door. It was during that time, one year after graduating high school, that I chose to accept Christ as my personal Lord and Savior. It was during a routine sales call that turned out to be anything but.

One day between stops, my sales partner asked me, "Ann, if you died today, do you know if you would go to heaven?"

Despite my belief about God and regular attendance at our neighborhood church, I really had no idea if I would be admitted into heaven. I answered

141

him honestly, and then he explained that according to the Bible, I could know for sure.

Miles Duley was a man who followed God's call on his heart, a call to witness, whenever and wherever possible.

We talked about what it meant to have a personal relationship with Jesus, to really be "saved." He shared that Jesus loved me unconditionally and wanted to have *every* part of me *all the time*, not just on Sunday at church. I liked the notion of being loved and accepted, and as we talked, I didn't think the life I was leading was one God would have thought acceptable.

When we are unsaved, we must realize we are standing at the crossroads of eternity and hell and awaken to God's gentle and persistent call to accept His gift of salvation.

On that day, I was ready to accept God's miraculous gift. I suddenly knew I wanted to change my life. I wanted the kind of salvation Miles said I could have.

When my sales partner pulled the car over to the side of the road to lead me in a simple prayer, I initially felt a little foolish. Praying out loud was completely foreign to me, but it also felt like the most natural thing I had ever done.

I admitted to God I was a sinner, which wasn't hard for me to do. I confessed I had tried to do my best but had fallen short. I asked for His forgiveness for my sin, acknowledged my faith in Jesus to save me, and asked Him to come into my life to be my Lord and Savior. A simple prayer (much like the one included in the previous chapter), combined with a genuine heart, completely changed the course of my life.

Scripture says, "If you confess with your mouth Jesus as Lord, and believe in your heart that God raised Him from the dead, you will be saved; for with the heart a person believes, resulting in righteousness, and with the mouth he confesses, resulting in salvation."[3]

Grasp God's Love for You

Today, Miles Duley is walking in the very presence of God, an opportunity he was always compelled to share with others. I'm forever grateful God equipped him with his fervent passion to share the hopeful and healing message of salvation whenever and wherever he was called. That day, it was in the front seat of his car on a city road in North Georgia during a routine sales call.

That day, I confessed my sins and accepted God's gift of salvation, a decision I grow more passionate about every single day.

I'm eternally thankful for Miles Duley, and I look forward to seeing him again one day.

4. *Surrendering to God.* Once we confess our sins and accept Christ as our personal Lord and Savior, our viewpoint changes—sometimes gradually, sometimes drastically—and we begin to walk out our sanctification, our spiritual growth, in the form of surrender.

Our ability to surrender is often hampered by our readiness and willingness to do so, as we often perch precariously on the fence between the two.

The majority of our lives as Christians is spent in this surrendering stage. This is the stage where we learn to measure our choices using God's plumb line. The stage where we learn to give up our own selfish desires that are not in alignment with God's and surrender to God's will, wants, and desires.

It's common in our culture today to do what makes us *feel* good, regardless of whether it's morally right or wrong. When we begin to understand why God placed restrictions on our behavior, we realize He created and stated moral standards in His Word for our protection. Sin will always take us farther than we want to go, keep us longer than we want to stay, and cost us more than we want to pay. Once we truly embrace this reality we will be much more apt to surrender to God's way of life, and in turn we will benefit through the blessings of greater peace, joy, hope, and happiness.

7 STEPS TO COURAGE

How God Sees Us

As we experience the four stages of how we see God, He is looking at us from four views as well. God knows all things at all times, and His view of us is four faceted:

1. He creates us.

2. He loves us.

3. He saves us.

4. He sanctifies us.

1. *He creates us.* The first facet of our journey as a child of God takes place before inception and continues throughout our childhood. God sees us as a creation in His image (Genesis 1:27); He knows us even before we are formed in our mother's womb (Jeremiah 1:5).

He searches us and knows when we sit and rise (Psalm 139:1–2); He discerns all our thoughts from afar (v. 2); He is intimately acquainted with all of our ways (v. 3); He knows every word we will say before we speak our first word (v. 4); He surrounds us with His protection (v. 5). He knows us so well there is no way we can comprehend it (v. 6).

2. *He loves us.* As we grow and begin to learn of His existence, the second facet of God's view of us is seen in the depth of His love for us, sinners and saints alike. His love for us is so vast it is beyond our understanding (Ephesians 3:19); it's a love so strong that He sacrificed His one and only Son so we might not perish but have eternal life (John 3:16).

3. *He saves us.* The third facet of God's view of us is seen through our salvation. Christ's finished work on the cross covers our sins with His blood so we can have eternal life. Once we place our faith in Christ, confess our sins, and

receive Him as our Lord and Savior, we are washed with pure water (Hebrews 10:22); we are a new creation; the old has passed away and the new has come (2 Corinthians 5:17). Our sins are blotted out (Acts 3:19), and we are free from them (Revelation 1:5). Therefore, God no longer sees us as the sinners we are; He sees Christ in us.

4. *He sanctifies us.* The fourth facet of how God sees us is viewed through our sanctification. We talked about this aspect in the chapter "The *R* Step in COURAGE." From the moment we surrender our life to Christ, we embark on our journey of sanctification, the process by which we are transformed to become more like Christ.[4] This is God's plan and perfect will for us (1 Thessalonians 4:3). Through sanctification, the Holy Spirit strengthens our ability to resist future sins by drawing us closer to Himself and to His Word. Think of this as the stage where God grows, nurtures, and sometimes prunes us.

Just like in the fourth stage of how we see God (when we're learning to surrender), this fourth facet of how God sees us (when we're learning how to become Christlike) is the place where we will spend the rest of our lives once we become believers.

GETTING TO KNOW GOD

When I asked the Lord to come into my heart and change me from within, I did not hear angels singing (although I now know they were). And honestly, I didn't really have a drastic, outward, life change. Some folks do; I just wasn't one of those folks. What did happen, however, was I began to have a growing awareness of God's presence in my life. But it wasn't until many years later that my transformed heart began to reflect a transformed life.

As a result of salvation, Christ's blood covers our sin, so we are cleansed and acceptable in the eyes our heavenly Father. But we must also realize that even after receiving salvation for our sins, we are still broken, sinful people in need of our Savior. Our brokenness doesn't simply go away. With the help of the Lord, we must begin to walk out our sanctification by growing in our fundamental spiritual health. For many of us, this can take years.

I spent the first twenty years of my salvation coasting along. There was no doubt I was saved, yet in many ways I was still lost. I didn't have someone in my life to disciple me or even encourage me to read and study God's Word. I didn't understand the importance or value of intentionally growing closer to God. I wasn't aware of the transformation that would take place as I strengthened my personal relationship with God and began to grasp His grace-filled love for me.

Getting to Know God's Word

One of the primary ways we get to know God is through studying and understanding His Word. Through the work of the Holy Spirit and our growth in the knowledge and understanding of God's Word, we are continually transformed into the women and men of God He calls us to be. When we neglect the intentional study of God's Word, as we discussed in the *R* step, we settle for spiritual growth that is slow and full of roadblocks. But when we study, understand, and apply God's Word to our lives, we begin to exchange a stagnant or slow-paced spiritual-growth journey for a steady and fulfilling one that will bring glory to God and transformation to our lives. "Sanctify them in the truth; Your word is truth" (John 17:17).

God drew me closer to Him when He introduced me to the in-depth study of His Word through Kay Arthur's Precept Ministries Bible study program.

Since that time, I have studied God's Word, book by book, and gained a greater understanding of who He is, how He interacts with us, what He desires for us, and, most importantly, how great and abundant His love, mercy, and grace are for us. Looking back, I realize now that God was clearly preparing my journey through the 7 Steps to COURAGE that was on my horizon. Author and pastor Warren Wiersbe said:

> The better you know your Bible, the better you will know yourself and what God wants to do for you. Also, the better you will know your Savior and what he can do to help make you a conqueror. Your Bible is God's gift to you (John 17:14) and, next to the gift of eternal life, it is the greatest gift you possess.[5]

Today, having studied, written, and taught the in-depth study of God's Word for more than a decade, I am convinced it is impossible to fully grasp God's love for us if we don't read, study, and strive to understand His Word.

I say this often: God's Word is transformational but only at the pace and depth to which we expose ourselves to it.

The topic of Bible study is broad. There are as many ways to teach it as there are to study it. For that reason, I've felt convicted to develop additional material that will be available on the In Grace Ministries website at www. InGraceMinistries.org.

FOUR BASIC STEPS TO BIBLE STUDY

In order to gain a proper understanding of the inspired writings of God, we must implement effective Bible study habits. Although I'm unable to fully explore this topic here, there are four primary steps to studying God's Word in depth:

1. Pray as we approach God's Word: Ask the Holy Spirit to guide us into all truth.

2. Observe God's Word: Ask the question, "What does the text say?"

3. Interpret God's Word: Ask the question, "What does the text mean?"

4. Apply God's Word: Ask the question, "What do I need to do?"

No matter what area of our lives God's instructions relate to, it's important to meditate on the lessons we learn in God's Word and allow the Holy Spirit to guide us in properly applying each lesson to specific areas of our lives (Bible study).

God's Word teaches us: "This book of the law shall not depart from your mouth, but you shall meditate on it day and night, so that you may be careful to do according to all that is written in it; for then you will make your way prosperous, and then you will have success."[6]

God's Love Revealed

I've been blessed to experience God's presence, power, and love throughout my life. One of the most profound times was when He took my mom home to be with Him.

It was a Monday morning in early May when my mom's caregiver called to tell me that Mom couldn't speak or respond. Her health had been deteriorating over the past six months, and doctors believed she was having ministrokes. Several times she had lost her ability to speak.

But this day was different, and we rushed her to the hospital. Within ten minutes of arriving in the emergency room, Mom had a grand mal seizure that put her in a coma.

For the next five days I spent virtually twenty-four hours a day by my mom's side. Her doctors were optimistic and her vital signs were good; she just wasn't waking up. When her neurologist asked if he could pray over her, I immediately said, "Yes!"

Grasp God's Love for You

Whether God chose to heal my mother on earth or by taking her to heaven, I had only one request from the doctor before he prayed: "Please pray for God's will to be done."

After he prayed and left the room, I sat in the chair next to Mom's bed and returned to reading God's Word to her.

The next morning in my quiet time as I sat next to my mother, I asked God for one thing: *Lord, if You decide to take Mom to heaven, please take her in such a way that I have no doubt it's You.*

As each doctor came in for rounds that morning, they consistently reported my mom's vital signs were strong; everything looked good. Her lungs, heart, kidneys, and virtually every organ looked good.

"Don't give up," her neurologist said. "She can still pull out of this."

I also learned that if she didn't, it could be weeks before her organs began to shut down. She could linger in this state for a long time.

A few hours after all of the doctors left, Mom's sister Pat (a registered nurse) arrived from North Carolina. I was thankful Aunt Pat was here to help. She was going to stay with Mom so I could go to the hotel next door to shower and take a quick nap. We talked quietly for a bit, and I stood at the end of Mom's bed before I walked out. She looked peaceful, but it was painful to see her so unresponsive.

"It's hard to see her like this," I said to Pat.

"I know, honey," she said softly, as she sat in the bedside chair.

Just as I got to the door, I felt compelled to turn around and look at Mom again. Something wasn't right. As I scanned her body, my eyes immediately went to her hands.

"Pat! Look at her hands," I said.

Before our very eyes, the color was draining out of my mother's hands. Her fingers, hands, and then wrists were gradually getting darker—they were turning blue. As we both watched in a kind of dumbfounded stupor, Mom's spirit left her body and she crossed over to heaven.

It happened just that fast.

The doctors were shocked at how quickly Mom passed away.

Tears streamed down my face as I recalled my morning prayer. God took my mother from this earth in a miraculous way, and I knew without any doubt He had taken her home. I never doubted God's love for Mom or me, but this experience solidified something even deeper in my soul, in my spirit.

How God's Love Changes Us

When my parents divorced, Mom moved in with us and Dad moved to California, where he eventually hit rock bottom. But he rebounded when he turned his life over to Christ at age sixty. During the final ten years Dad had left on this side of heaven, he became a different person. His strength was no longer a liability; from that point on he found his strength in Christ.

Shortly after making his decision, Dad shared his letter to God with me. It is one of my most treasured earthly possessions.

While the *G* step in COURAGE had yet to be created, I nonetheless experienced both of my parents' grasp of God's love for us. For that supreme honor, I am truly blessed.

It can take some of us a lifetime to grasp God's love for us. The wonderful blessing is that it's never too late to do so. God's love, mercy, and grace are available right here, right now. Today.

DAD'S LETTER TO GOD

DEAR GOD;
  IT is NOW 12:10 A.M. ON APRIL 14th. iN
THE YEAR, OF YOUR LORD JESUS 1986. I
ON This DATE DO ACCEPT YOU AS MY
SAVIOR . YOU ARE NOW iN COMPLETE
CONTROL AND I WiLL LOOK TO YOU
FOR LEADERSHiP. WHERE YOU LEAD I
WiLL FOLLOW. IT is MY UNDERSTANDING
THAT YOU hAVE FORGIVEN ME FOR ALL
MY SiN. AND WRONG DOiNGs. FROM This
DAY FORWARD I AM CLEAN.
                          Sincerely
                          Arnold

151

COURAGE CALL-TO-ACTION STEPS

1. Take out your notebook or journal and write down how you see God.

2. Write down how you believe God sees you. Reference Scripture to support your view.

3. Now write down the stage you believe you are in on your spiritual growth journey: seeing, believing, accepting, or surrendering. Write out what stage you would like to see yourself grow into. Then pray and ask God for wisdom and guidance in achieving your spiritual goals.

4. Pray about the importance of studying God's Word. Write down a challenge you are willing to take in order to improve your knowledge and understanding of Scripture. For example, "I will commit to a daily reading routine." Or maybe, "I am going to join a Bible study."

9

E Step in Courage:
Embrace a Life of Grace

Courage is giving grace to those who have hurt us.

"From His fullness we have all received, grace upon grace."
—John 1:16 ESV

*g*race is an extravagant gift from God, a gift many of us find extremely difficult to understand, let alone accept and embrace.

Grace is God's unfathomable gift of love, favor, kindness, mercy, and forgiveness. It's the root of our faith. It grounds us and reminds us we have a loving heavenly Father who sympathizes with our weaknesses and struggles. God's grace washes us clean and removes every particle of our sin from His sight.

While it is God's desire that we extend grace to others, when the word is used in connection with Him, it takes on a more powerful meaning. God desires to be reconciled with the crown of His creation—you and me. The sin separating us from our Creator must be overcome, and God's grace makes it possible.

The best way to fully embrace God's gift of grace is to set aside our need to hold on to our mistakes, our sin. We need to unpack our negative baggage and willingly accept His gift without self-condemnation or guilt. Without fear, shame, hurt, or sin. Just draw near to Him, as Scripture promises:

> We do not have a high priest who cannot sympathize with our weaknesses, but One who has been tempted in all things as we are, yet without sin. Therefore let us draw near with confidence to the throne of grace, so that we may receive mercy and find grace to help in time of need.[1]

Together, we have walked through the first six steps to courage. While every step to this point can be life changing, this seventh and final step in our courage journey can be transformative. When we truly embrace a life of grace, it can give birth to an internal awareness of the presence of God that will completely alter our life.

EXTRAVAGANT GRACE

The theme of reconciliation between God and humankind is woven throughout Scripture. God loves us and wants to save us from a life in bondage to sin. He demonstrates this desire in every aspect of the birth, life, death, and resurrection of His one and only Son, Jesus Christ.

God, through His extravagant compassion for you and me, became fully human in Jesus. Born in a manger to Mary and Joseph, and as the son of a carpenter, Jesus lived a humble life. He grew into a natural-born leader and a brilliant teacher of God's Word. He eventually revealed His true identity, was baptized by John the Baptist, and through the indwelling of the Spirit of God became God in the flesh. Kissed by Judas, Jesus felt the sting of betrayal and experienced the powerlessness of abuse. He was beaten and then crucified on the cross; He conquered death and was resurrected from the grave. Jesus provided loving guidance for His followers in that He left us His Word and sent the Holy Spirit for our sanctification.

Through the gospel of Christ, God extended His promise to us as believers that through grace we might experience healing for our broken hearts and freedom from our bondage to sin.

Jesus Christ is the grace-filled answer and ultimate expression of God's passionate desire to save us from ourselves. He paid the ultimate price for our sin out of the richness of God's grace.

This familiar acronym is often used to explain grace:

God's
Riches
At
Christ's
Expense

© InGraceMinistries.org

7 STEPS TO COURAGE

RESISTING GRACE

At salvation, I embraced Christ's acceptance of me, yet I still had a hard time embracing the fact my failures were no longer a part of my identity. It took almost three decades after praying to receive Christ before I understood I was actually resisting God's grace. His grace was available all along, but it couldn't fully impact my life until I learned to fully embrace it. My Savior covered my sin and shame, but my inner judge still worked overtime delivering messages to the contrary. I just couldn't grasp what God was offering.

During the first six months of counseling, working to save a marriage that remained connected by the grace of God, I was challenged repeatedly by my counselor to lay aside my need to hold on to my failures and embrace God's grace-view.

"But what about . . . ," I would say.

"Christ covered that too," my counselor would respond.

If we resist embracing God's grace, we hold on to failures that become easy darts for Satan to repeatedly use against us.

RECEIVING GRACE

Sin holds each of us captive before salvation. After receiving God's grace-filled gift of salvation, sin no longer has a grip on us, unless we choose to allow it.

Author Max Lucado says, "Grace comes after you. It rewires you. From insecure to God secure. From regret riddled to better because of it. From ready to die to ready to fly. Grace is the voice that calls you to change and then gives you the power to pull it off."[2]

The apostle Paul urged us *not* to receive the grace of God in vain (2 Corinthians 6:1).

Embrace a Life of Grace

Grace is not an abstract quality, but a dynamic, active, working principle: "For the grace of God has been revealed, bringing salvation to all people. And we are instructed to turn from godless living and sinful pleasures" (Titus 2:11–12, NLT). It is not some kind of ethereal blessing that lies idle until we appropriate it. Grace is God's sovereign initiative to sinners (Ephesians 1:5–6).

In his book, *The Gospel According to the Apostles*, author John MacArthur talks about the modern view of grace using the term coined by Dietrich Bonhoeffer: *cheap grace.*

Bonhoeffer defined cheap grace this way:

> The preaching of forgiveness without requiring repentance, baptism without church discipline, communion without confession, absolution without personal confession. Cheap grace is grace without discipleship, grace without the cross, grace without Jesus Christ, living and incarnate.[3]

Bonhoeffer's point is that grace is meant to justify the sinner, not the sin, yet many Christians take it to mean, "I can sin because of grace."[4]

MacArthur says:

> Many professing Christians today utterly ignore the biblical truth that grace "instruct[s] us to deny ungodliness and worldly desires and to live sensibly, righteously, and godly in the present age" (Titus 2:12).
>
> Instead, many people live as though grace is a Get Out of Jail Free card, a no-strings-attached, open-ended package of amnesty, beneficence, indulgence, forbearance, charity, leniency, immunity, approval, tolerance, and self-awarded privilege divorced from any moral demands.[5]

Once we are saved, we are a new creation; old things have passed away and new things have come.[6] Therefore, in order to keep God's grace from being in vain, as Paul warned, we must embrace it fully, do away with shame and self-condemnation, turn away from our sin, be reconciled to God, and pursue a life worthy of His amazing grace.

The hymn "Amazing Grace," written in 1779 by John Newton, is one of the most popular spiritual songs of all time. Newton's early years consisted of tragedies, trials, poor choices, and bad behavior.

Newton's life change came on March 10, 1748, when a slave ship he was traveling on encountered a severe storm and almost sank. In his distress, Newton cried out to God and converted to Christianity. Immediately following his spiritual rebirth, he stopped drinking, gambling, and cursing. He eventually became a priest, wrote hymns for his services, and later collaborated with a poet to write and publish a volume of hymns, which included the familiar and beloved "Amazing Grace":

Amazing Grace, how sweet the sound,
That saved a wretch like me.
I once was lost but now am found,
Was blind, but now I see.

Anyone who truly embraces God's grace can't help but be moved by this beautiful hymn. The Bible says, "But by the grace of God I am what I am, and His grace toward me did not prove vain; but I labored even more than all of them, yet not I, but the grace of God with me."[7]

Embrace a Life of Grace

Giving Grace

God's Word commands us to "see to it that no one comes short of the grace of God; that no root of bitterness springing up causes trouble."[8] In other words, we have a responsibility as believers to care for one another. God freely and abundantly offers us grace. In turn, we must freely and abundantly offer grace to others.

For a long season, I was incapable of genuinely giving grace to others. While I found it increasingly easy to share God's message of unconditional forgiveness and grace with those struggling with fear, shame, hurt, and sin, I found it much harder to extend that same message of forgiveness and grace to people who had offended me.

But God has a way of convicting our spirit when He wants us to change. Especially as we begin to accept the things we cannot change and find the courage to change the things we can. God used Ephesians 4:29 to help me grow: "Let no unwholesome word proceed from your mouth, but only such a word as is good for edification according to the need of the moment, so that it will give grace to those who hear."

Over time, I became more aware of my need to extend grace, and I've learned to catch myself when I am in situations where my grace is tested.

Do you struggle at times to extend grace? Do you wonder what extending grace really looks like in real life?

I was given an assignment in a seminary class to randomly witness to strangers and journal my experiences. With my busy schedule, I waited until the day before the assignment was due to begin. In a hurry and with the assignment looming over my head, I had errands to run and three stops to make. My first stop was my wireless carrier. I waited my turn, and as I approached the desk, a disgruntled employee greeted me. I politely made my request, and without a kind word the sales associate attempted to fix the problem with my phone. My first thought was, *I guess I won't be striking up a conversation with this person.*

Then God softly reminded me to consider grace. In a matter of seconds, I was challenged to consider the possibility that something in this salesperson's life was at the root of her attitude. So I extended grace in the form of kind words and compliments. Within seconds her demeanor changed, she opened up, and it seemed as though our conversation brightened her day. I was even able to share my faith with her, and she opened up about hers. On my next two stops, I had very similar experiences.

How often do we get caught up in our busy lives and neglect to recognize the needs of others? When we run across people with bad attitudes or who are just downright rude, we have the choice to respond with grace. We all possess the ability to extend grace, but are we ready and willing to do so on a moment's notice?

When Mike and I were going through our marital crisis, we experienced many highs and lows; times when we had breakthroughs that made us hopeful and happy and times when setbacks left us feeling hopeless and hurt. One of the hardest things to do is to extend grace to someone who has hurt you, but grace was exactly what Mike and I had to learn to extend to each other.

Consider the hurt and pain we cause God when we blatantly sin against Him, when we turn our backs on Him and choose our ways over His ways. Yet His grace is unconditional and unending. He is moved by compassion for our sinful state and is always willing to forgive *and forget.*

Are we willing to do the same?

In Grace

Grace is not a one-time, name-it-and-claim-it event in the Christian experience. We stand in grace (Romans 5:2). The entire Christian life is driven and

160

empowered by grace: "It is good for the heart to be strengthened by grace, not by foods" (Hebrews 13:9). God says we should "grow in the grace and knowledge of our Lord and Savior Jesus Christ" (2 Peter 3:18).

Several months after I took the first step to courage in my hotel room in Israel, I sensed the Lord leading me to develop an outreach ministry.

"A what?" I remember asking God. "Am I hearing You correctly, Lord?"

I was passionate about God's Word, enthusiastic about teaching the Bible, and I couldn't deny my heart for broken and hurting people, but what did that have to do with a full-time ministry? Mike and I were deep into individual and couples counseling; surely, this wasn't the time to begin to think about starting a nonprofit ministry. How could I possibly be the spokesperson for anything at this point?

In my spirit, I thought I heard God sigh at that very moment as I was reminded of how many times He had to repeat His call to Moses to be His spokesman. On the heels of that gentle reminder, I suddenly remembered a time when I prayed to God on my knees after an argument with Mike, a time when God impressed on my heart that one day I would be His spokesperson.

COMFORTING REASSURANCE

I know the exact date because I wrote it in the margin of my Bible: December 12, 1998. Mike and I were skiing in Colorado with friends. We had gotten into a fight, and I stayed back at the condo while everyone else went skiing. I needed to pull myself together and handle my emotions. I prayed while tears ran down my face. I hated being at odds with Mike; I hated how empty I felt. Then, at that very moment, I received a promise from God. As I grabbed my Bible to read, it fell open to Jeremiah 15:19–21.

I read verse 19: "If you return, then I will restore you—Before Me you will stand; and if you extract the precious from the worthless, you will become My spokesman. They for their part may turn to you, but as for you, you must not turn to them."

At the time, I had no idea what this message meant to Jeremiah, but I knew exactly what it meant for me. God was encouraging me to return my focus to Him, to allow Him to restore my hope, heal my emotions, and fill the emptiness in my heart. God was asking me to concentrate on my relationship with Him and allow Him to heal my relationship with Mike. And, I clearly understood there was a future involved—one where I would become God's spokesperson, a person others would turn to—but in the meantime, I must be mindful of Whom and what I follow.

Reading on in verse 20, God gave me the reassurance I needed: "Then I will make you to this people a fortified wall of bronze; and though they fight against you, they will not prevail over you; for I am with you to save you and deliver you."

In my moment of pain, God was offering me more than just comfort. He was offering me protection and a promise I could draw courage from. No matter how defeated I felt, He would strengthen me, protect me from those who fight against me, and see me through the hard times. But most of all, God promised me I would never be alone. He was with me, no matter what.

I had no way of knowing what God had in store for me as I sat in that condo in Colorado and prayed, but I was comforted by His instructions and promises. I had no idea God would take the next fourteen years to prepare me to be his spokesperson in ways I never dreamed. And I had no idea He was systematically walking me through seven steps that would change my life and eventually become the book you are reading today.

Embrace a Life of Grace

SURRENDERING TO GOD'S CALL

Years later as I began to pray about the ministry God was encouraging me to develop, I knew it had to represent the foundation of my healing, and the hope I passionately wanted to share with others. I knew right away it had to center around grace, the gift God had granted me that allowed me to move past my pain and find the courage to go forward.

Today, In Grace Ministries is flourishing, with a mission to strengthen, equip, and empower people with God's message of comfort, hope, and salvation. And even more important, my marriage has reached a miraculous point of restoration I never believed possible. The Lord taught me: "'My grace is sufficient for you, for power is perfected in weakness.' Most gladly, therefore, I will rather boast about my weaknesses, so that the power of Christ may dwell in me."⁹

God's grace is abundant and available to us all. His love and comfort are waiting patiently for us as we seek to find comfort in the people, places, and things of this world. Our most courageous action is to relinquish our need for control and rest in the loving arms of our Lord and Savior, Jesus Christ. Only then will we find true comfort, a comfort we will want to shout about to everyone we meet.

God's grace, love, and mercy can't be contained—they must be shared.

As we come to this final step in our COURAGE acrostic, I pray you will choose to embrace the fullness of God's plans and purposes for your life and that you will joyfully accept the gift of abundant grace He longs for us all to have.

Our heavenly Father desires nothing more than for us to receive His grace. He wants to heal our hurts, remove our fears, and restore our hope. He wants to give us grace, comfort, and peace to face life with courage so we, too, can comfort and encourage others in the same way we are comforted.

The Bible says, "Grace to you and peace from God our Father and the Lord Jesus Christ. Blessed be the God and Father of our Lord Jesus Christ, the Father of mercies and God of all comfort, who comforts us in all our affliction so that we will be able to comfort those who are in any affliction with the comfort with which we ourselves are comforted by God." [10]

COURAGE CALL-TO-ACTION STEPS

1. Take out your notebook or journal and write at least a paragraph about what it means to you to embrace God's grace.

2. Ask God to reveal trigger situations in your life where your ability to extend grace is often tested, and write them down.

3. Ask God to reveal people in your life who need to receive grace from you. Write down their names and at least one way you could extend grace to them. Then pray for each one.

4. Write down a specific action plan for intentionally embracing and extending grace. Commit to implementing your plan and then journal your progress.

10

Move Forward in Freedom

Courage is choosing to persevere even when we are afraid.

"You will know the truth, and the truth will make you free."
—John 8:32

*F*reedom means something different to each of us. To some, it may mean eliminating debt, overcoming relational issues, or no longer allowing people, pressures, and past pain to steal their joy. To others, freedom could mean escaping an abusive relationship, conquering an addiction, or being able to freely follow Christ without having to worry about repercussions.

To me, freedom means making choices based on faith rather than on fear. It means laying down masks, embracing openness and honesty, and seeing my value in God's eyes. It means establishing safeguards to help me resist temptations and pursuing God-given opportunities to share my story, faith, and the gospel with others. In my new, courageous world, freedom also means no longer riding an emotional roller coaster in my marriage and enjoying a healthier, more grace-filled relationship with my husband.

7 STEPS TO COURAGE

The Bible says, "Now the Lord is the Spirit, and where the Spirit of the Lord is, there is freedom."[1]

It takes courage to move forward in freedom, courage we gain through implementing each step in the 7 Steps to COURAGE. Moving forward in freedom doesn't happen overnight. It's a process, one that involves intentional prayer and planning. From the first step to the last, we must lean into our relationship with God, trust He is in control, and yield everything to Him.

This is the essence of what it means to let go and let God.

MOVING FORWARD

Congratulations for getting through the 7 Steps to COURAGE! As you work to incorporate the COURAGE acronym into your daily life, there are a few additional steps you can take to remove any lingering restraints and completely move forward in freedom:

1. Resist Satan.

2. Extend forgiveness.

3. Grow friendships.

4. Improve communication.

5. Develop perseverance.

1. Resist Satan

"He has shown you, O mortal, what is good. And what does the LORD require of you? To act justly and to love mercy and to walk humbly with your God."[2]

Christ died to set us free: free from the penalty of sin and free from everlasting separation from God. When we truly embrace freedom, we must no longer allow ourselves to be torn down by the Four Pests of Pressure, to be barricaded by obstacles, isolated by masks, or misled by lies.

As we begin to implement the courage steps on a daily basis, it's important to understand the limitations of our enemy, Satan.

Satan can't control us, but he can persuade us.

He can't read our minds, but he can put thoughts in them.

Therefore, our job is to recognize his schemes, resist his temptations (James 4:7), and take captive our thoughts to the obedience of Christ (2 Corinthians 10:5).

Jesus said, "The thief comes only in order to steal and kill and destroy. I came that they may have and enjoy life, and have it in abundance [to the full, till it overflows]."[3]

Our counselor encouraged Mike and me to use one helpful exercise when negative thoughts and temptations come to mind. We are to ask ourselves, is this thought from God or Satan? As simple as this may sound, it has become an intentional, healthy habit that helps me to rationally act, rather than emotionally react.

2. Extend Forgiveness

One of the greatest struggles I had with forgiveness involved forgiving myself. Sure, it can be hard to forgive others, but for me, I've always found it just as difficult to forgive myself. How about you? Does this sound familiar? When we've allowed the Four Pests of Pressure to eat away at our fundamental foundations of strength and self-esteem, it gets pretty easy to beat ourselves up.

As I have grown closer to God in my walk with Him, I have learned the key to forgiving myself and others is fully receiving God's gracious forgiveness. "Bearing with one another, and forgiving each other, whoever has a complaint against anyone; just as the Lord forgave you, so also should you."[4]

Let's take a look at what forgiveness is and what it is not.

Forgiveness is canceling a debt owed, no longer focusing on the wrong done, letting go of negative thoughts and feelings, and viewing the offender with acceptance and compassion.

Extending the grace to forgive requires that we first allow God to heal the pain that came from the offence. Grace is needed for both healing and forgiveness. When we truly forgive from the heart, we are able to see other people in terms of their need rather than their sin.

Forgiveness is not the same as reconciliation. Reconciliation requires two parties. An offender needs to take responsibility for his or her wrongs, ask for forgiveness, and work to rebuild trust. The offended person may need time to see the fruit of change before he or she is able to fully reconcile with an offender.

When we work to resolve an unforgiving spirit, we must consider both sides of the coin. Not only do we need to deal with forgiving those who have offended us, we must also ask forgiveness from people we have offended.

As Mike and I worked to overcome years of hurt, we learned that simply saying "I'm sorry" didn't cut it. We had to learn a much more effective way to apologize.

When we are young and disobey our parents, we are often told to say, "I'm sorry." A mother may say, "Now, son, tell your sister you're sorry." But the little boy may fight and fidget until his mom is compelled to say, "Son, I mean it. Tell your sister you're sorry." Finally, the little boy voices those two simple words, "I'm sorry," realizing he must do as he is told in order to continue playing with his toys and avoid further punishment.

Have you ever watched a scenario like this and grimaced at the child's lack of genuine remorse?

But how often do we, as grown adults, do the same thing?

Move Forward in Freedom

For years, to avoid conflict and to keep the peace, I was quick to apologize and say "I'm sorry" without really being broken or remorseful for what I had done. As I have grown in my relationship with the Lord, and with the help of our Christian counselor, I've come to realize there is a big difference between a simple "I'm sorry" and an "I was wrong. Will you forgive me?" The biggest difference in these two approaches is an attitude of the heart.

If our goal is to be truly courageous, we must reach this point of heart-change.

King David wrote Psalm 51 as a prayer for forgiveness after being confronted for his adultery with Bathsheba. As I studied this psalm, I reflected on the remorse and brokenness David expressed to God as he cried out for cleansing and reconciliation.

Are we, like David, deeply sorry for what we've done? Do we genuinely ask for forgiveness from God and others when we sin against them? When we are open and honest with God about our sin, we are more likely to be open and honest with others.

Therefore, ask God for forgiveness, approaching Him with the humility He desires (Psalm 51:16–17). Call on His lovingkindness and compassion (v. 1), and ask Him to cleanse you of your wrongdoing (vv. 2–4).

And remember to forgive those who have hurt or offended you. God is just, and He will deal with their punishment. It's time to let it go.

Author Warren W. Wiersbe said:

If you take care of yourself and walk with integrity, you may be confident that God will deal with those who sin against you. Above all, don't give birth to sin yourself; rather, pray for those who persecute you. God will one day turn your persecution into praise.[5]

3. Grow Friendships

You've likely heard "You are what you eat" and "You are who you hang around with." There's a lot of truth in these pithy statements.

We talked about the importance of building healthy, safe relationships in "The *O* Step in COURAGE: Overcome Obstacles." In our journey to walk in grace, it's important to surround ourselves with supportive and encouraging friends. Having healthy relationships can help us move forward in freedom. On the other hand, when we have consistently negative or energy-sapping individuals in our life, we can find ourselves in emotional bondage that makes everything harder than it has to be.

This doesn't mean we are to cast aside every challenging or dysfunctional relationship in our lives. It means we need to pray for wisdom and discernment concerning our interpersonal relationships and work to make them better as we make ourselves better. Unfortunately, in some instances being able to move forward in true freedom does mean separating ourselves from some people—particularly toxic people. But that's an extreme measure that needs to be approached with care and prayer. In many cases, all it takes to change the dynamics of a relationship is a change in perspective, a different communication style, or perhaps the establishment of healthier boundaries.

While growing friendships can certainly mean expanding our circle of influence by meeting new people, it can also mean changing the dynamics in existing relationships by taking off our masks and uncovering our true selves.

When we share our fears, pain, and needs with people we can trust, and we realize others have been through some of the same trials, we feel less alone. There is such incredible freedom in realizing we are not alone.

Two of the most powerful words we can share with one another are simply *Me too.*

Move Forward in Freedom

Even God shares our experiences. By becoming fully human, He personally understood poverty, felt the sting of betrayal, and experienced the powerlessness of abuse.

Be prayerful in how you approach communicating with people in your circle of influence. In the process of moving forward in freedom, we must be considerate of others who may be affected by our courageous pursuit of freedom. It's important we are careful not to run over others while exercising our newfound freedom. I completely understand the euphoric feelings that begin to multiply when we start to strut with courageous confidence—when we know we are walking in God's will and purpose. It's something we want to share with everyone—why would they not want to hear our excitement and feel like this?

Alas, just because you are ready to commit to change, overcome your obstacles, and uncover your true self doesn't mean everyone around you feels likewise. There is no doubt in my mind God knows exactly what He's doing, especially if He has placed challenging people in your life. Your ability to truly influence the people around you will be dependent on your ability to walk the talk before you talk the walk (if you get my drift).

4. Improve Communication

Learning new communication skills was vital in my courage walk. The consequences of ineffective communication can significantly damage—or even destroy—a relationship. When it comes to being courageous, it is wise not to undervalue the importance of learning how to communicate.

Playwright George Bernard Shaw said, "The single biggest problem in communication is the illusion that it has taken place."

Are you really ready to make fearless choices and walk in grace? Are you ready to leave behind the stress of living in fear and move boldly forward in courage? If so, a critical component of all seven steps to courage is being able to communicate with others in a healthy way.

There are two major players important in communication: the person speaking and the person listening.

There's a big difference between speaking in truth and love and speaking in anger and judgment. Likewise, there's a big difference between simply hearing and actually listening.

Hearing is perceiving sound. Listening, on the other hand, speaks of our ability to pay attention to someone in order to hear and understand what is being said.

Author Stephen R. Covey said, "Most people do not listen with the intent to understand; they listen with the intent to reply."[6]

If we desire to truly communicate well with others, we must listen rather than simply hear what they are saying. Attentive listening is vital in establishing a safe and healthy environment for communication. If we are quick to interrupt, change the subject, or invalidate someone's thoughts, beliefs, or feelings, we will likely establish negative barriers in the relationship that will hinder self-expression.

Jesus Christ came to set us free, and He took our place on the cross. We don't have to hide behind guilt, shame, or fear. We don't have to feel isolated or suffer alone.

The Bible says, "It was for freedom that Christ set us free; therefore keep standing firm and do not be subject again to a yoke of slavery."[7]

When we talk about relational problems (one of the key areas in the Four Fundamental Foundations of Health), communication (or the lack thereof) is a significant factor.

Move Forward in Freedom

We generally learn our communication skills as children through the examples of others. In healthy families, good communication becomes the norm; in dysfunctional families, negative or no communication skills are built.

Words can be helpful or hurtful, and it's critically important to our emotional and relational health to engage in regular checkups to assess how our own words and the words of others are affecting our hearts and minds.

At times, we are often so consumed with our need to speak, we barely let others get their words out before we jump in with our insights and opinions. Other times, we are so consumed with how we are going to respond, we neglect to listen to what is actually being said.

This happens quite often in relationships, and unfortunately it shuts down communication.

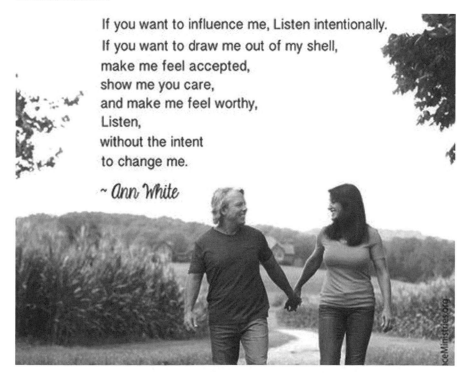

If you want to influence me, Listen intentionally.
If you want to draw me out of my shell,
make me feel accepted,
show me you care,
and make me feel worthy,
Listen,
without the intent
to change me.

~ Ann White

Our goal in communication should be to encourage others to share their thoughts, opinions, and beliefs rather than to discourage them from opening up. We need to be aware of these four main conversation killers:[8]

1. *Criticism.* This is a negative verbal response we often use when we disagree, disapprove, object, or judge others' thoughts or actions. God's Word reminds us to speak the truth in love (Ephesians 4:15), not truth in criticism. This requires that we think before we speak and speak in a grace-filled way that communicates our nonjudgmental position of what we believe to be the truth, realizing we may or may not be correct in our perception of the truth.

2. *Defensiveness.* We often employ a verbal reaction when someone disagrees, disapproves, objects, or judges us. Defensiveness puts up a wall in the midst of a conversation. It generally responds with an attack of the other person, and it's an easy way to begin a deadly conversational cycle that gets us nowhere but dizzy.

The best way to change this pattern of communication is to ask, "Is there anything I am being criticized for that has any merit?" If so, take ownership and muster up the courage to respond by thanking them for their opinion and owning any part of the wrongdoing. If not, consider responding with, "I appreciate your being honest about how you feel," and avoid the temptation to defend yourself.

3. *Contempt.* This is a nonverbal or verbal expression of disgust or dislike. It can be as simple as rolling your eyes at another person. Overcoming contempt requires you to deal with your anger and to practice expressing care and gratefulness for the other person, even in the midst of conflict. This requires intentional focus on God's will, complete control of emotions, and grace for the other person.

4. Stonewalling. This is a refusal to communicate, either by giving the silent treatment or by ignoring another person. It's refusing to consider another person's perspective. Some people stonewall to protect themselves, while others simply employ it out of anger.

As in every obstacle we face, we must identify and deal with any underlying fear, shame, hurt, or sin that is contributing to any breakdown in communication.

We must continually strive to speak, listen to, and approach communication in healthy, productive, and grace-filled ways.

All that said, it means we need to act rationally and not respond emotionally.

Oh my goodness, how is that possible?

5. Develop Perseverance

Perseverance can be defined as "one's ability to keep trying, to endure, and to maintain patience through difficult circumstances and/or suffering." When facing a challenge, setback, or even unavoidable failure, perseverance gives us the ability to push through any situation and continue moving forward toward a more prosperous and productive future.

The Bible says, "We are afflicted in every way, but not crushed; perplexed, but not despairing; persecuted, but not forsaken; struck down, but not destroyed."[9]

Throughout life, we encounter or hear about individuals who face and overcome insurmountable difficulties. These people seem to share a quality that helps them become survivors instead of victims. When all is said and done, *perseverance* is the best word to capture this quality, which includes faith, endurance, hope, and a hearty dose of courage.

7 STEPS TO COURAGE

In his book *Abounding Grace,* author Scott M. Peck wrote:

Perseverance does not come naturally, but rather we must strive to obtain, strengthen, and exercise perseverance throughout life. Perseverance is considered "the great virtue of seeing things through" and comes from the Latin prefix *per,* meaning "by" or "through" and the Latin word *severus,* meaning "severe" or "strict."[10]

In other words, courageous spiritual maturity is produced by going through the severe difficulties of life, not in having the difficulties eliminated from life.

In his book *Three Steps Forward, Two Steps Back: Persevering Through Pressure,* author and beloved pastor Chuck Swindoll says:

God does not offer a formula that produces fully mature Christians overnight. Christian growth comes through hardcore, gutsy perseverance (a forgotten word!) of applying what you hear and obeying it . . . and thereby learning how to handle those inevitable problems.[11]

When I think back on the years I spent in bondage to fear, shame, hurt, and sin (the Four Pests of Pressure), I cringe at the memory.

Today, I am nothing like that fearful woman.

Today, God has given me a passionate desire to share the truth of His Word that transformed my life.

As you walk through your personal journey to find courage, I pray you will be open to sharing your story with the people God places in your life. The apostle Peter tells us we were chosen by God "to do his work and speak out for him, to tell others of the night-and-day difference he made for you."[12]

Move Forward in Freedom

Today, we have many powerful examples of individuals triumphing over tremendous obstacles, becoming bright beacons of light to shine God's love, mercy, and grace on people who are suffering. These good examples include Mother Teresa, Bethany Hamilton, Amy Purdy, and Joni Eareckson Tada. We've got profoundly transparent contemporary Christian authors writing serious books about suicide, depression, adultery, abortion, abuse, and boundaries. Authors like Kay Arthur, Beth Moore, Allison Bottke, Elizabeth George, Carol Kent, Don Piper, Rick Warren, John Townsend and Henry Cloud, to name a few. Because of their willingness to expose deeply personal and painful issues, these authors have provided us with powerful resources that ultimately contribute to our ability to develop a deeper understanding of who we are—and Whose we are.

In his acclaimed book, *Mere Christianity*, C. S. Lewis wrote, "God knows our situation; He will not judge us as if we had no difficulties to overcome. What matters is the sincerity and perseverance of our will to overcome them."[13]

JESUS, THE ULTIMATE EXAMPLE OF PERSEVERANCE

Our greatest example of perseverance is found in our Lord and Savior, Jesus Christ. We place our confidence in His endurance to finish the work of our salvation through His death, burial, resurrection, and ascension, providing us access to God.

In Philippians, Paul beautifully portrayed Christ's attitude of perseverance to accomplish our salvation as the ultimate example. When we strive to be Christlike and respond to our circumstances with persistent faithfulness, God can accomplish His transformative work in us.

As we implement courage steps that may usher us into profound seasons of change, let's draw upon the strength of God just as those who have gone before us and have persevered in trials both great and small. When we are faced with challenging, fearful, depressing, or overwhelming circumstances, let's look to God's Word for comfort, guidance, and wisdom.

Together, let's choose to persevere and endure whatever hardships may come our way. And remember, Scripture never implies that perseverance is entirely dependent on human efforts alone. God empowers Christians to move forward in freedom, persevere through life, and even rejoice when their lives bring God glory through enduring severe difficulties.

God's Word encourages us to persevere, and He promises us an amazing gift when we reach the end of the race: "Blessed is a man who perseveres under trial; for once he has been approved, he will receive the crown of life which the Lord has promised to those who love Him."[14]

COURAGE CALL-TO-ACTION STEPS

1. Take a moment to pray about circumstances where you are in need of God's empowerment to help you resist Satan, extend forgiveness, grow friendships, improve communication, or persevere. Ask God to use your life circumstances to develop these areas in your life and ultimately bring Him glory.

2. Take out your notebook or journal and write down at least one goal for each of the five steps for moving forward in freedom, listed at the start of this chapter. Develop a plan to implement these goals in the coming week.

3. Ask God for wisdom and discernment concerning areas in your life where you need to move forward in freedom. Write down the areas He reveals and pray over them daily over the next week.

11

Find Joy in the Journey

Courage is choosing joy in the midst of all circumstances.

"May the God of hope fill you with all joy and peace as you trust in him,
so that you may overflow with hope by the power of the Holy Spirit."
—*Romans 15:13* NIV

J've been blessed throughout my life to enjoy many happy times; great times with family and friends, memorable holidays, fabulous vacations, and so much more. However, as happiness came and went over the years, it became apparent to me something was missing. It took me a long time to realize that "something" was joy.

I discovered happiness is temporary; it's a feeling that comes from pleasure in the moment, experiencing accomplishments, or having a desire met. Joy, on the other hand, is more than a feeling. It's a state of mind that stems from a close, personal relationship with God. True joy is grounded in faith, trust, and hope. Ultimately, it is found in the promises of God.

7 STEPS TO COURAGE

The Bible tells us God wants to clothe us in beauty rather than in ashes; He wants us to feel joy rather than to mourn and to offer praise rather than despair.[1]

Joy can be a constant thread that runs throughout our lives regardless of our present circumstances. If our joy is grounded in God and our eternity, nothing can take it away. People can't take it away and Satan can't steal it; we are the only ones who can choose to push it aside. Sadly, we can sometimes be our own worst enemy when it comes to claiming God's promises.

Joy is a choice. It's choosing to celebrate the blessings in life rather than focusing on the difficulties. It's choosing to trust God with our problems, believing that no matter what, everything is going to be okay, regardless of our circumstances. True joy comes when we walk with courageous purpose. No matter what we are going through, finding joy on the journey is always an option.

God Is in Control

There is a plaque on my kitchen windowsill that consistently reminds me of God's sovereign control over my life. It reads:

"Good morning, this is God. I will be handling all of your problems today."

This visual reminder convicts me regularly that if I give my worries and concerns to God, and trust Him with the outcome, I have a greater ability to overcome the obstacles in life and embrace joy. It reminds me of who is really in control.

There were times on my journey through the 7 Steps to COURAGE when I had to force myself to focus on joy rather than on despair. At times I felt completely alone, hopeless about the future of my family, and overwhelmed from the weight of processing past hurts. But through the process, I learned to trust God with the outcome. I learned to focus on what I could find joy in: my relationships with my children, my grandchildren, friends, and family. I learned to appreciate my health and the health of those I love. I especially learned to appreciate my close relationship with God and His promise that everything I was going through would somehow work together for good.[2]

Appreciating what we have plays a significant part in our ability to walk in grace and to find joy in our journey.

While this might sound like cliché advice, it's nonetheless true. Being thankful at all times is critical to maintaining a healthy balance in life, particularly in the midst of storms.

I came across the following anonymous quote during my courage journey, and it stopped me in my tracks: "The things we take for granted someone else is praying for."

Seriously, I had to stop and immediately ask myself what it is I am focused on, and what do I take for granted that someone else may be desperately asking God for in prayer?

It didn't take me long to realize I was so wrapped up in trying to fix what wasn't going right in my life, there was little to no room left to consider what was going right. Can you relate? Do you find it easy to get caught up in trying to fix what's not going your way and take for granted the many blessings that surround you?

These days, I intentionally set aside time each morning to thank God for all the blessings in my life. Sure, there are things I wish I wasn't going through or didn't have to deal with, but in reality I can think of plenty of things I am grateful for.

If we stop and take the time, we can all think of things we should be more grateful for. They're very likely things other people are praying for right this very moment.

I am reminded to "rejoice always; pray without ceasing; in everything give thanks; for this is God's will for you in Christ Jesus."[3]

IT'S ALL ABOUT PERSPECTIVE

When we take time every day to adopt an attitude of gratitude, it shines through in our personality, outlook, performance, and relationships. It helps to give us the courage to make choices that aren't always easy.

It sounds strange—backward even—but sometimes it takes an intentional effort on our part to recognize the struggles other people are going through in order to find joy in our own journey.

With our busy schedules and multitudes of distractions, we rarely stop to think about what is going on halfway around the world or even halfway across town.

But that wasn't the case for me when I visited India on a mission trip and saw firsthand what was going on halfway around the world. My family was back home in Georgia, and while I would never diminish their personal struggles, I knew their lives were nothing like what I witnessed in the towns we visited.

In many places I visited, I saw people persevering in grim circumstances.

My heart broke as I listened to their stories, stories of immense poverty, physical and sexual abuse, and of young girls being sold into slavery for barely more than a bottle of alcohol.

At the same time, I heard stories of hope from many of the same suffering people. Stories of men, women, and children being saved and lives being transformed as a result of God's amazing grace.

The evidence of God's light was everywhere there, just as Jesus said, "I am the Light of the world; he who follows Me will not walk in the darkness, but will have the Light of life."[4]

Find Joy in the Journey

Everywhere we turned in India we encountered light and hope in the realization that salvation is attainable, and a real relationship with the one true God is available to those who choose to repent and believe. In places where despair once reigned, there is now a presence of God's Holy Spirit bringing hope and restoration to the hearts and souls of these gracious—and grateful—people.

I met many women and men whose lives and families are being transformed as a result of their salvation, and the light of Christ is shining in and through their lives. I met a young girl who lives and works in the red-light district who prayed to receive Christ. She learned she is unconditionally loved and cared for by her Lord and Savior, in spite of the profession she is trapped in. I met children who have been rescued from brothels and are now being raised in Christian homes where hope and healing are experienced daily.

My personal struggles seemed slight in comparison. Being able to witness this level of courageous living gave me a decidedly different perspective on what it means to make fearless choices and truly walk in God's grace. It gave me an ability to feel joy deep in my spirit.

You may never have the opportunity to see what life is like in other parts of the world, but the truth is, God is shining His light all around the world, including right here in our own backyards. It takes courage to recognize the good and appreciate our blessings—however large or small—in difficult times. Yet it's this perspective that will bring us true joy.

DARE TO DREAM

Dreams help us to focus on the future, to see beyond our current circumstances into the possibilities of what can be. We develop dreams, visions, and ambitions at all stages of life. They are an integral part of the direction our lives take. Our dreams often represent the calling God has placed on our life.

7 STEPS TO COURAGE

Bruce Wilkerson, author of *The Dream Giver*, has this to say about pursuing our dreams:

> The journey toward your Big Dream changes you. In fact, the journey itself is what prepares you to succeed at what you were born to do. And until you decide to pursue your Dream, you are never going to love life the way you were meant to.[5]

Unfortunately, many of us abandon our dreams when fear-based choices strangle our hopeful ambitions.

Sometimes other people discourage us from our dreams, and sometimes the Four Pests of Pressure are responsible for eroding our aspirations. If we ignore or suppress our dreams long enough, they will simply become distant memories stuffed in the recesses of our minds and will never have the opportunity to be realized. No matter our age, background, or circumstances, we should all be encouraged to pursue our dreams.

God has God-sized dreams for us if we are willing to move beyond where we are. If we set aside time with the Lord, He will begin to reveal where He wants to take us. One important element in analyzing our dreams is to put them in perspective by asking ourselves if this dream is based on something we believe God wants us to do. Or is this dream based on selfish desires?

God's dreams are beyond what we can think or imagine. He is the One who can open the doors to our dreams if we are willing to submit to His plans and allow Him to lead.

NEW BEGINNINGS

Our God is a God of second chances and new beginnings.

Throughout my lifetime, I have been given second chances in relationships, occupations, education, ministry, and so much more. God walked me through the 7 Steps to COURAGE over the course of several years. As a result of consistently applying these steps, I have been given second chances to forgive, to overcome my negative attitudes, behaviors, and coping skills, and to choose obedience to God. Today, I find great joy in having the kind of relationships and life I've always dreamed of.

We serve a God of justice who allows consequences, testing, and tribulation to shape us into the people He wants us to be. He is also longsuffering, patient, kind, and forgiving, and He doesn't desire for any of His children to suffer. He wants us to do well.

God's repeated call for repentance throughout Scripture beautifully represents His desire to give every one of us a second chance. "If we confess our sins, He is faithful and righteous to forgive us our sins and to cleanse us from all unrighteousness." [6]

Let today be the day you choose to rediscover your purpose, reclaim your dreams, and find amazing grace and hopeful joy in your life journey. The Bible says, "A cheerful heart is good medicine, but a broken spirit saps a person's strength." [7]

PASSIONATE PURPOSE

When Rick Warren's landmark book, *The Purpose Driven Life*, released, it seemed everyone was reading it, myself included. He struck a chord with his message when he said, "God gives us different passions so that everything he wants done in the world will get done." [8]

With a passionate desire to help us understand why we are alive and know God's amazing plan for us, both here and now, and for eternity, Rick Warren encouraged us with this blueprint for Christian living in the twenty-first century—a lifestyle based on God's eternal purposes, not on cultural values.

7 STEPS TO COURAGE

If you haven't read this book, I encourage you to do so now. If you have read it, I encourage you to dust off your copy and read it again.

On our journey to live courageously, *The Purpose Driven Life* is a great resource—particularly during the *U* step in COURAGE: Uncover your true self. Actually, this is a great resource through all seven steps, because the process of walking through these COURAGE steps is often painful. It takes tremendous fortitude to embark on this trip, and without a clear vision of our purpose, it's sometimes difficult to weather the storms of change.

But as Rick Warren says, it's often the storms of life that enable us to ultimately find courage:

> God uses problems to draw you closer to himself. The Bible says, "The LORD is close to the brokenhearted; he rescues those who are crushed in spirit."[9] Your most profound and intimate experiences of worship will likely be in your darkest days—when your heart is broken, when you feel abandoned, when you're out of options, when the pain is great— and you turn to God alone. It is during suffering that we learn to pray our most authentic, heartfelt, honest-to-God prayers. When we're in pain, we don't have the energy for superficial prayers.[10]

CHOOSE JESUS

Finding courage, making fearless choices, and walking in grace means freedom. Freedom from the emotional baggage you once lugged around.

You have the freedom to commit to change and overcome obstacles that threaten your peace. You're free to find your true identity in Christ as you uncover your true self and replace worldly lies with scriptural truth. Free to accept the things you cannot change as you grasp God's love for you and embrace a life of grace. By implementing these seven steps, we can find fearless freedom to be the people God is calling us to be—to walk in His purpose for our lives.

As we reach the end of our journey together, my prayer is that you let today be the day you begin to replace fear with faith, let go of your negative habits, and walk in intentional courage. If you haven't done so already, let today be the day you take that important first step to courage and commit to change. Let today be the day you embrace your God-given gifts and opportunities and step out in faith, believing God has a purpose and great plans for your life.

It's time to be courageous—to stop being afraid.

It's time to choose Jesus—and joy.

Choose Dreams

We all have the same amount of time in a day, but it's how we steward our time that matters. If you take the time to dream, consult God regarding your dreams, set goals, clear away the obstacles, and begin to put a plan in place, you will be amazed at what dreams God will lead you to realize in your life.

As a matter of fact, you may be surprised when God opens unexpected doors to dreams you never thought were possible. That's been my experience in recent years as I've walked in courage and embraced grace and joy. My courage and healing opened me up to a newfound ability to say yes to God.

As I've dreamed and prayed for ways to serve Him and encourage others, God has opened doors to learning, missions, speaking, leading, and teaching. God has given me opportunities to speak into the lives of others around the world, and He has ushered me into an arena only He could prepare me for. This shy, insecure, fearful girl now embraces the courage to cohost a Christian talk show, author the first of what I pray will be many books, and develop Bible studies to encourage and empower fellow believers around the world.

There is no expiration date on achieving the dreams of your heart.
God can always make a way when there seems to be no way.

Choose Joy

Joy can be found in every phase of your journey. It's not something you have to wait to achieve once you've righted every wrong, processed every hurt, or fixed every problem. It can be achieved by choosing to acknowledge it, by focusing on God's promises and sovereignty, and by implementing positive daily routines that usher in joy.

"Instruct those who are rich in this present world not to be conceited or to fix their hope on the uncertainty of riches, but on God, who richly supplies us with all things to enjoy."[11]

Life can be hard; some days harder than others. But God wants us to enjoy life, and true joy and enjoyment are possible when we embrace His gifts and blessings.

As we say good-bye, I urge you to be intentional in developing your foundation of joy. It can be one of the most important ingredients that allow you to persevere in your journey to make courageous choices and embrace God's compassionate love and grace.

To God be the glory, great things He has done—and continues to do! In grace and love, I remain, as always, your sister in Christ,

COURAGE CALL-TO-ACTION STEPS

1. Pray and ask God to open your eyes to joy.

2. Take out your notebook or journal each day for the next ten days and write down at least five things you are thankful for. Thank God for them, and let them be the foundation of your joy throughout each day. (Consider doing this every day from now on. You will be amazed at the difference it will make in your perspective.)

3. In your notebook or journal, write down your dreams. Pray over them and ask God to reveal His dreams and purpose for you.

4. Commit today to write out your goals on how you intend to implement the 7 Steps to COURAGE into your daily life.

THE 7 STEPS TO COURAGE

Commit to Change

Overcome Obstacles

Uncover Your True Self

Replace Worldly Lies with Spiritual Truth

Accept the Things You Cannot Change

Grasp God's Love for You

Embrace a Life of Grace

© InGraceMinistries.org

Notes

Introduction
1. Romans 8:1.
2. James 5:16, ESV.

Chapter 1
1. Ephesians 3:20, NLT.
2. Psalm 37:4.
3. Matthew 6:33.
4. 2 Corinthians 5:17.
5. Joel 2:25.
6. June Hunt, *Counseling Through Your Bible Handbook* (Eugene, OR: Harvest House Publishers, 2008), 37.
7. Leland Ryken et al., *Dictionary of Biblical Imagery* (Downers Grove, IL: InterVarsity Press, 2000), 176.

Chapter 2
1. Romans 12:2.
2. See Matthew 14:24–31.
3. Hebrews 12:2, HCSB.
4. 1 Thessalonians 5:23.
5. "Do not be bound together with unbelievers; for what partnership have righteousness and lawlessness, or what fellowship has light with darkness?" (2 Corinthians 6:14).

Chapter 3
1. Matthew 7:3, AMP.
2. Philippians 2:1–4.
3. Ephesians 2:8–9.

4. Alex Lickerman, MD, "The Two Kinds of Beliefs," *Psychology Today*, April 24, 2011, https://www.psychologytoday.com/blog/happiness-in-world/201104/the-two-kinds-belief.

5. 1 John 4:1.

6. "The Benefits of Physical Activity," Centers for Disease Control and Prevention, 2/4/15, http://www.cdc.gov/physicalactivity/basics/pa-health/index.htm#ImproveMentalHealth.

7. John P. Schuster, "The Gift of Disassociation," *Psychology Today*, December 6, 2013, https://www.psychologytoday.com/blog/the-power-your-past/201312/the-gift-disassociation

8. James 1:14–15, ESV.

9. See Philippians 4:19.

10. Francis Chan with Danae Yankoski, *Crazy Love: Overwhelmed by A Relentless God* (Colorado Springs: David C. Cook, 2013), 63.

11. John 16:33.

12. Matthew 19:26.

Chapter 4

1. Matthew 11:28–30.

2. Warren W. Wiersbe, *Be Strong*, BE Commentary Series (Wheaton, IL: Victor Books, 1996), 43.

3. Hebrews 13:6.

4. Brené Brown, *Daring Greatly: How the Courage to Be Vulnerable Transforms the Way We Live, Love, Parent, and Lead* (New York: Penguin Group Publishers, 2012), 69.

5. Brené Brown, *Daring Greatly*, 66.

6. G. L. Welton, "Conflict Management," ed. David G. Benner and Peter C. Hill, *Baker Encyclopedia of Psychology & Counseling*, Baker Reference Library (Grand Rapids, MI: Baker Books, 1999), 247.

7. Melody Beattie, *Codependent No More: How to Stop Controlling Others and Start Caring for Yourself* (Center City, MN: Hazeldon, 1986, 1992), 34.

8. Melody Beattie, *Codependent No More*, 3.

9. Ephesians 4:26–27.

10. Proverbs 18:1, ESV.

11. Ecclesiastes 4:9–12.

12. Philippians 4:6, NIV.

13. 1 Chronicles 16:11.

14. Ephesians 4:31–32.

15. Hebrews 12:15.

Notes

16. Michael D. Lemonick, "How We Get Addicted," Time, 7/5/2007, www.wiphl.com/uploads/media/TIME-addiction.doc.
17. Ibid.
18. Malachi 2:16, amp.

Chapter 5
1. See Acts 5:29.
2. Proverbs 27:19, NIV.
3. Psalm 139:23–24.
4. Proverbs 28:13, NKJV.
5. 2 Corinthians 5:17.
6. 1 John 4:9.
7. June Hunt, *Counseling Through Your Bible Handbook* (Eugene, OR: Harvest House Publishers, 2008), 355.
8. Albert Bandura, "Social Learning Theory," Learning Theories.com, http://www.learning-theories.com/social-learning-theory-bandura.html.
9. Peter Scazzero, *Emotionally Healthy Spirituality: It's Impossible to Be Spiritually Mature While Remaining Emotionally Immature* (Grand Rapids, MI: Zondervan, 2006), 11.
10. Robert H. Mounce, *Romans: The New American Commentary*, vol. 27 (Nashville: Broadman & Holman Publishers, 1995), 167.

Chapter 6
1. Brené Brown, *Daring Greatly: How the Courage to Be Vulnerable Transforms the Way We Live, Love, Parent, and Lead,* (New York: Penguin Group Publishers, 2012), 216.
2. Psalm 12:6; Proverbs 30:5.
3. Chicago Statement on Biblical Inerrancy with Exposition 1978 Article XII, http://www.bible-researcher.com/chicago1.html.
4. Josh McDowell and Bill Wilson, *A Ready Defense: Over 60 Vital "Lines of Defense" for Christianity Topically Arranged for Easy Reference* (Nashville: Thomas Nelson Publishers, 1993), 27–28.
5. Eugene E. Carpenter and Philip W. Comfort, *Holman Treasury of Key Bible Words: 200 Greek and 200 Hebrew Words Defined and Explained* (Nashville: Broadman & Holman Publishers, 2000).
6. Hosea 4:6.
7. Peter Scazzero, *Emotionally Healthy Spirituality: It's Impossible to be Spiritually Mature While Remaining Emotionally Immature* (Grand Rapids, MI: Zondervan, 2006), 185.

8. Dr. Chris Thurman, *The Lies We Believe* (Thomas Nelson, Kindle Edition, 2003).

9. Bruce A. Little, "The Formation of Belief," BeThinking.org, http://www.bethinking.org/truth/the-formation-of-belief.

Chapter 7

1. Reinhold Niebuhr, "The Serenity Prayer," Wikiquote, https://en.wikiquote.org/wiki/Reinhold_Niebuhr.

2. Romans 3:23.

3. 1 Timothy 4:16.

4. Luke 6:37.

5. 1 Thessalonians 5:14, italics mine.

6. Daniel 2:21.

7. Ephesians 5:15–16.

Chapter 8

1. Romans 8:31.

2. Romans 15:13.

3. Romans 10:9–10.

4. Eugene E. Carpenter and Philip W. Comfort, *Holman Treasury of Key Bible Words: 200 Greek and 200 Hebrew Words Defined and Explained* (Nashville: Broadman & Holman Publishers, 2000).

5. Warren W. Wiersbe, *A Gallery of Grace: 12 New Testament Pictures of the Christian Life* (Grand Rapids, MI: Kregel Publications, 1988, 2002), 118.

6. Joshua 1:8.

Chapter 9

1. Hebrews 4:15–16.

2. Max Lucado, *Grace: More Than We Deserve, Greater Than We Imagine* (Nashville: Thomas Nelson, 2014), [page?].

3. Bryan Galloway, "The Third Reason Dietrich Bonhoeffer Can Impact Us: Costly Grace," BonhoefferBlog, https://bonhoefferblog.wordpress.com/the-third-reason-dietrich-bonhoeffer-can-impact-us-costly-grace/.

4. Jon Walker, *Costly Grace: A Contemporary View of Bonhoeffer's "The Cost of Discipleship"* (Abilene, TX, Leafwood Publishers, 2010), 19.

5. John MacArthur, "What Is Grace?" Grace to You with John MacArthur, http://www.oneplace.com/ministries/grace-to-you/read/articles/what-is-grace-10339.html.

Notes

6. See 2 Corinthians 5:17.
7. 1 Corinthians 15:10.
8. Hebrews 12:15.
9. 2 Corinthians 12:9.
10. 2 Corinthians 1:2–4.

Chapter 10
1. 2 Corinthians 3:17, ESV.
2. Micah 6:8, NIV.
3. John 10:10, AMP.
4. Colossians 3:13.
5. Warren W. Wiersbe, *Prayer, Praise, & Promises: A Daily Walk Through the Psalms* (Grand Rapids, MI: Baker Books, 2011), 22.
6. Stephen R. Covey, *The 7 Habits of Highly Effective People* (NY: Simon & Schuster, 1989), 229.
7. Galatians 5:1.
8. Drs. John and Julie Gottman refer to these four conversation killers as the "Four Horseman" and offer valuable insight into these relational predators. For more information, visit http://www.gottman.com.
9. 2 Corinthians 4:8–9.
10. Scott M. Peck, *Abounding Grace: An Anthology of Wisdom* (Kansas City, MO: Andrews McNeal Publishing, 2000), 133.
11. Charles R. Swindoll, *Three Steps Forward, Two Steps Back: Persevering Through Pressure* (Nashville: Thomas Nelson Publishers, 1990), 18.
12. 1 Peter 2:9, MSG.
13. C. S. Lewis, *Mere Christianity*, revised and amplified ed. (New York: Harper Collins Publishing, 1980), 99.
14. James 1:12.

Chapter 11
1. See Isaiah 61:3, NIV.
2. See Romans 8:28.
3. 1 Thessalonians 5:16–18.
4. John 8:12.
5. Bruce Wilkerson, with David and Heather Kopp, *The Dream Giver: Following Your God-Given Destiny* (Colorado Springs, CO: Multnomah Books, 2003), 76.
6. 1 John 1:9.
7. Proverbs 17:22, NLT.

NOTES

8. Rick Warren, The Purpose Driven Life (Grand Rapids, MI: Zondervan, 2002), 293.
9. Psalm 34:18, NLT.
10. Rick Warren, *The Purpose Driven Life* (Grand Rapids, MI: Zondervan, 2002), 194.
11. 1 Timothy 6:17.

Resources for Help

The National Domestic Violence Hotline: Check out www.thehotline.org or 1-800-799-7233 (or 1-800-787-3224 for TTY): Call for help in a crisis or for assistance in developing a safety plan. Staffed twenty-four hours a day, 365 days a year.

American Association of Christian Counselors: Visit www.AACC.net for help in finding a professional Christian counselor.

Recommended Reading

Marriage/Relationships

1. Allison Bottke, *Setting Boundaries with Difficult People: Six Steps to Sanity for Challenging Relationships* (Eugene, OR: Harvest House Publishers, 2011).
2. Daniel B. Wile, *After the Fight: Using Your Disagreements to Build a Stronger Relationship* (New York: The Guilford Press, 1993).
3. Douglas Rosenau, *Slaying the Marriage Dragons: Protecting Your Marriage from the Enemies of Intimacy: Busyness, Little Neglects, Passive Husbands & Angry Wives, Affairs, Codependent Craziness, Poor Communication* (Wheaton, IL: Victor Books, 1991).
4. Dr. David and Teresa Ferguson and Dr. Chris and Holly Thurman, *Intimate Encounters: A Practical Guide to Discovering the Secrets of a Really Great Marriage.* (Cedar Park, TX: Relationship Press, 1997).
5. Gary Chapman, *The 5 Love Languages: The Secret to Love That Lasts* (Chicago: Northfield Publishing, 1992, 1995, 2004).
6. Dr. Henry Cloud and Dr. John Townsend, *Boundaries: When to Say Yes, When to Say No to Take Control of Your Life* (Grand Rapids, MI: Zondervan, 1992).
7. Dr. Henry Cloud and Dr. John Townsend, *Safe People: How to Find Relationships That Are Good for You and Avoid Those That Aren't* (Grand Rapids, MI: Zondervan, 1992).
8. Howard J. Markman, Scott M. Stanley, and Susan L. Blumberg, *Fighting for Your Marriage* (San Francisco: John Wiley & Sons, Inc. 2010).
9. Jeff VanVonderen, *Families Where Grace Is in Place: Building a Home Free of Manipulation, Legalism, and Shame* (Bloomington, MN: Bethany House Publishers, 2010).

10. John Gottman, PhD, and Nan Silver, *What Makes Love Last? How to Build Trust and Avoid Betrayal* (New York: Simon and Schuster, 2012).

11. John Gottman, PhD, and Nan Silver, *The Seven Principles for Making Marriage Work: A Practical Guide from the Country's Foremost Relationship Expert* (New York: Crown Publishers, Inc., 1999).

12. Leslie Vernick, *How to Act Right When Your Spouse Acts Wrong* (Colorado Springs, CO: WaterBrook Press, 2001).

13. Leslie Vernick, *The Emotionally Destructive Relationship: Seeing It, Stopping It, Surviving It* (Eugene, OR: Harvest House Publishers, 2007).

14. Patricia Evans, *The Verbally Abusive Relationship: How to Recognize It and How to Respond* (Avon, MA: Adams Media, 2010).

15. Robin Junes Gunn, *Victim of Grace: When God's Goodness Prevails* (Grand Rapids, MI: Zondervan, 2013).

Overcoming Destructive Emotions

16. Allison Bottke, *Setting Boundaries for Women: Six Steps to Saying No, Taking Control and Finding Peace* (Eugene, OR: Harvest House Publishers, 2013).

17. Brené Brown, PhD, LMSW, *Daring Greatly: How the Courage to Be Vulnerable Transforms the Way We Live, Love, Parent, and Lead* (New York: Penguin Books Ltd., 2012).

18. Dr. David Hawkins, *When Pleasing Others Is Hurting You: Finding God's Patterns for Healthy Relationships* (Eugene, OR: Harvest House Publishers, 2004).

19. Dr. Henry Cloud, *Changes That Heal: The Four Shifts That Make Everything Better . . . And That Anyone Can Do* (Grand Rapids, MI: Zondervan, 1990–92).

20. Francine Shapiro, PhD, *Getting Past Your Past: Take Control of Your Life with Self-Help Techniques from EMDR Therapy* (New York: Rodale Inc., 2012).

21. June Hunt, *Counseling Through Your Bible Handbook* (Eugene, OR: Harvest House Publishers, 2008).

22. Kay Porterfield, *Violent Voices: 12 Steps to Freedom from Emotional Abuse and Verbal Abuse* (Deerfield Beach, FL: Health Communications, Inc., 1989).

23. Les Carter and Frank Minirth, *The Anger Workbook: A 13-Step Interactive Plan to Help You Understand How Unmet Needs Can Feed Anger* (Nashville: Thomas Nelson, Inc., 1993).

Recommended Reading

24. Mary DeMuth, *Not Marked: Finding Hope and Healing After Sexual Abuse* (Rockwall, TX: Uncaged Publishing, 2013).

25. Melody Beattie, *Codependent No More: How to Stop Controlling Others and Start Caring for Yourself* (Center City, MN: Hazelden Foundation, 1986).

26. Patrick J. Carnes, PhD, *The Betrayal Bond: Breaking Free of Exploitive Relationships* (Deerfield Beach, FL: Health Communications, Inc., 1997).

27. Peter A. Levine, PhD, *In an Unspoken Voice: How the Body Releases Trauma and Restores Goodness* (Berkley, CA: North Atlantic Books, 2010).

28. Stephen Arterburn, *Healing Is a Choice: Ten Decisions That Will Transform Your Life & Ten Lies That Can Prevent You from Making Them* (Nashville: Thomas Nelson, 2005).

Spiritual and Emotional Growth

29. Charles Swindoll, *The Grace Awakening: Believing in Grace Is One Thing, Living It Is Another* (Nashville: Thomas Nelson, 2010).

30. Max Lucado, *Grace: More Than We Deserve, Greater Than We Imagine* (Nashville: Thomas Nelson, 2012).

31. Bruce Wilkerson, with David and Heather Kopp, *The Dream Giver: Following Your God-Given Destiny,* (Colorado Springs, CO: Multnomah Books, 2003).

32. Carol Kent, *Between a Rock and a Grace Place: Divine Surprises in the Tight Spots of Life* (Grand Rapids, MI: Zondervan, 2010).

33. Peter Scazzero, *Emotionally Healthy Spirituality: Unleash a Revolution in Your Life in Christ* (Nashville: Thomas Nelson, 2006).

34. Richard A. Swenson, MD, *The Overload Syndrome: Learning to Live Within Your Limits,* (Colorado Springs, CO: NavPress, 1998).

35. Robert Morris, *From Dream to Destiny: The Ten Tests You Must Go Through to Fulfill God's Purpose for Your Life* (Ventura, CA: Regal Books/Gospel Light, 2005).

About the Author

Ann White is a native Carolina girl, who met her husband and soul mate shortly after moving to Atlanta in 1978. She founded In Grace Ministries out of a calling on her life to share with others how God and His Word brought restoring truth to her life. Ann is an author, speaker, teacher, and short-term missionary.

For years Ann's heart has been burdened for those who need to hear God's Word and are suffering due to circumstances beyond their control. Having personally experienced God's grace, salvation, and life-changing power, Ann has a desire to extend this same love, mercy, and encouragement to others, so they, too, may be reconciled to God.

On top of being a wife, a mom, a grandmother, and leading a ministry, Ann co-hosts Atlanta talk show *Atlanta Live*, and is currently pursuing her master's degree at Southeastern Baptist Theological Seminary.

Despite her busy schedule, most days you can find Ann spending quiet moments with the Lord, hanging out with her husband, boys, and their families, working out, writing, reading, enjoying friends, and living *in grace*.

You can connect with Ann on her social media sites:

ingraceministries.org  /AnnWhiteIGM  /AnnWhiteIGM

ABOUT IGM

For many years, Ann's heart has been burdened to share God's love with others. Having personally experienced God's grace, salvation, and the life-changing power of His Word, Ann's greatest desire is to extend this same love, mercy, and encouragement to others, so they too, may be reconciled to God.

Ann founded In Grace Ministries (IGM), a non-profit organization (501c3) that is dedicated to helping people grow in their personal relationship with God by strengthening believers, equipping ministry leaders, and empowering women and children at risk. IGM is currently in the process of producing and publishing inspirational books, bible studies and leadership curriculum that encourage people to embrace the transformed life Christ offers.

Through local and international missions, speaking engagements, social media, and Christian television programing, IGM reaches countless men, women, and children with God's message of inspiration, encouragement, and hope.

Strengthening Believers, Equipping Leaders, Empowering Women and Children At Risk

ingraceministries.org  /AnnWhiteIGM 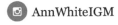 AnnWhiteIGM